CAMBRIDGE

T0303164

AMERICAN EMPOWER

WORKBOOK WITH ANSWERS

B1

PRE-INTERMEDIATE

Peter Anderson

CONTENTS

1A DO YOU PLAY ANY SPORTS?

1 VOCABULARY Common adjectives

a Underline the correct words to complete the sentences.

1 The new building in front of the university is *rude* / *ugly* / *all right*. I hate it!
2 Our new teacher is always very *serious* / *silly* / *rude*. We work very hard in her class, and she never smiles or laughs.
3 The cakes at the new bakery are *silly* / *serious* / *delicious*!
4 My brother's new girlfriend is *ugly* / *beautiful* / *delicious*. I think she's a model.
5 We played a lot of *silly* / *horrible* / *perfect* games at Sarah's birthday party. I have some really funny photos on Facebook.
6 Lily's a *perfect* / *strange* / *wonderful* person. Her grandchildren love visiting her.

b Complete the sentences with the adjectives in the box.

~~boring~~ all right awful amazing delicious rude strange perfect

1 I'm not interested in soccer. It's so boring.
2 Thanks for the chocolates. They were ________!
3 Look at this beautiful weather – it's a ________ day to go to the beach.
4 The movie we saw last night was really ________. I didn't understand it at all.
5 **A** How was the restaurant?
B Oh, it was ________. There are better Italian restaurants in my town.
6 The weather in Seattle was ________. It rained every day.
7 The band was ________! It was the best concert I've ever been to.
8 The server at the hotel was ________. He said he couldn't help us because we're vegetarian.

2 GRAMMAR Question forms

a Underline the correct words to complete the questions.

1 How many children *he does have* / *does he have* / *does have he*?
2 Where *did you meet* / *did meet you* / *you met* your husband?
3 *Did he grow up* / *He grew up* / *He did grow up* in this area?
4 What *was like the movie* / *was the movie like* / *the movie was like*?
5 How much *paid you* / *you did pay* / *did you pay* for your smartphone?
6 *Why she go* / *Why she went* / *Why did she go* to the U.S.?
7 How many movies *he made* / *did he make* / *did make he* last year?
8 How *was your vacation* / *your vacation was* / *did your vacation be*?

b Put the words in the correct order to make questions.

1 you / Sarah's friend / are ?
Are you Sarah's friend?
2 work / a bank / he / does / in ?
____
3 you / last month / to New York / go / did / why ?
____
4 like / that new Brazilian / what / restaurant / is ?
____
5 with your sister / who / that man / was ?
____
6 TV shows / you / do / watch / what kind of ?
____
7 go to / did / which university / you ?
____
8 did / how much / cost / the tickets ?
____

1B I'M REALLY INTO SOCIAL MEDIA

1 VOCABULARY Adverbs

a Put the words in parentheses in the correct place in each sentence.

1 They see their grandchildren now that they live in Australia. (hardly ever)
They hardly ever see their grandchildren now that they live in Australia.
2 I enjoy watching old Hollywood movies. (particularly)
____
3 She hates it when people are late for meetings. (absolutely)
____
4 We go to Italian restaurants, but sometimes we go to Mexican ones. (usually)
____
5 We're sure his flight arrives at terminal 2, but I need to check. (pretty)
____
6 I hope he brings his beautiful sister to the party! (really)
____

b Underline the correct adverbs to complete the sentences.

1 I love rock music, but I *absolutely* / *especially* / *fairly* like the Foo Fighters. They're my favorite band.
2 He *hardly ever* / *never* / *especially* calls his mother – maybe once or twice a month.
3 I *rarely* / *pretty* / *usually* enjoy horror movies, but this one was awful!
4 She's *fairly* / *absolutely* / *rarely* good-looking, but I don't think she's beautiful.
5 I *never* / *really* / *hardly ever* hate math. I just don't understand it!
6 She *usually* / *particularly* / *rarely* takes her family out for dinner – only when it's her birthday.
7 They love all sports, but they're *fairly* / *really* / *pretty* interested in baseball. They watch all the games on TV.
8 It's *pretty* / *usually* / *rarely* cold today, so why don't you take your gloves?

2 PRONUNCIATION Long and short vowels

a 01.01 Listen to the words. Do the letters in **bold** make long or short vowel sounds? Check (✓) the words with long vowel sounds.

1 ☑ b**a**nk
2 ☐ **aw**ful
3 ☐ p**er**fect
4 ☐ m**u**sic
5 ☐ **u**gly
6 ☐ h**o**tel
7 ☐ **o**ften
8 ☐ arr**i**ve
9 ☐ **u**niversity
10 ☐ f**a**vorite

3 GRAMMAR Simple present and present continuous

a Underline the correct verb forms to complete the sentences.

1 She *is loving* / *loves* / *love* reading fashion magazines at the hairdresser's.
2 We usually *are going* / *goes* / *go* to the café across from the hotel.
3 I *'m reading* / *read* / *reading* a great book in English right now.
4 He *'s wanting* / *does want* / *wants* to call his family in Tokyo. Can he use the Wi-Fi?
5 Why *are you waiting* / *do you wait* / *you waiting* for the bus? Let's walk home.
6 I hardly ever *am visiting* / *visit* / *visits* my cousins in Ireland.
7 She *studies* / *studying* / *'s studying* French politics at college this semester.
8 Yes, they're here. They *play* / *'re playing* / *playing* a video game in the living room.

b Complete the conversation with the simple present or present continuous forms of the verbs in parentheses. Use contractions where possible.

MEGAN What [1] 's Andrea doing (Andrea, do) in that store?
NAOMI She [2] __________ (buy) some postcards to send to her family.
MEGAN Really? I [3] __________ usually [4] __________ (not send) postcards. I usually [5] __________ (write) a message on Facebook. And sometimes I [6] __________ (post) a few photos of my vacation on Instagram.
NAOMI Yes, me too, but Andrea's grandparents [7] __________ (not use) social media, so she [8] __________ (send) them postcards instead.
MEGAN Oh, and what [9] __________ (Marco and Jack, do) this morning?
NAOMI They [10] __________ (spend) the day at the beach.
MEGAN But Marco [11] __________ (not like) swimming in the ocean. He says the water's too cold.
NAOMI Yes, but it [12] __________ (be) really hot today!

c 01.02 Listen and check.

1C EVERYDAY ENGLISH
It was really nice to meet you

1 USEFUL LANGUAGE
Greeting people; Ending conversations

a Underline the correct words to complete the conversation.

SAM Hi, James! 1 *Much / Long / Very* time no see! How are you?
JAMES Hi, Sam. I'm fine, thanks. 2 *What a / What / How* nice surprise! Great to see you!
SAM Yes, it's really nice 3 *see you / to see you / you see*, too.
JAMES Where are you living 4 *today / this day / these days*?
SAM Oh, not 5 *far from / far of / far away* here. On Park Road, near the baseball stadium.
JAMES Oh, 6 *what / how / who* nice!
SAM And 7 *she is / it is / this is* my wife, Jess.
JAMES Your wife – wow! That's wonderful 8 *new / news / notices*! Nice to 9 *meet / meat / meeting* you, Jess.
JESS Nice to meet you, 10 *two / too / to*.

b 01.03 Listen and check.

c Complete the sentences with the words in the box.

surprise	hello	meet	news	again
time	last	~~nice~~	need	call

1 Sea View Road? Oh, how nice !
2 Your husband – wow! That's wonderful ______!
3 I really ______ to go. I'm late.
4 What a nice ______!
5 Say ______ to Carlos for me.
6 Long ______ no see!
7 It was really nice to ______ you.
8 I'll give you a ______.
9 It was great to see you ______.
10 When did we ______ see each other?

d 01.04 Listen and check.

2 PRONUNCIATION
Sentence stress

a 01.05 Listen to the sentences and underline the stressed words.

1 I'm pretty sure it was two months ago.
2 What a nice surprise!
3 It was really nice to meet you.
4 I'm sorry, but I really need to go.
5 Where are you living these days?
6 I'm late for a meeting.

1D SKILLS FOR WRITING
I'm sending you some photos

1 READING

a Read Nandeep's email to Hannah and check (✓) the correct answer.

a ☐ Nandeep is staying at the Taj Mahal hotel in Delhi.
b ☐ Nandeep is visiting his cousins in Boston.
c ☐ Nandeep is on vacation at his aunt and uncle's house in Delhi.

b Read the email again. Are the sentences true or false?

1 Nandeep mainly speaks in Hindi to his cousins.
2 He's visiting a lot of places while he's in India.
3 The Taj Mahal is in Delhi.
4 Nandeep didn't enjoy visiting the Taj Mahal.
5 Nandeep often uses his aunt and uncle's pool.
6 Nandeep isn't enjoying his vacation.

Hi Hannah,

I hope you're enjoying your stay in Boston.

I'm spending a month in India on vacation. I'm staying with my aunt and uncle and my two cousins in Delhi. I don't speak much Hindi, but they all speak English very well, so communication isn't a problem. They're taking me to see a lot of really interesting places. Yesterday we drove to Agra and visited the Taj Mahal. It took two hours to get there. This is a photo I took – what an amazing building!

It's really hot here all the time, but my aunt and uncle have a swimming pool, so we spend a lot of our time in the water – it's so relaxing! In the evenings, I usually go to cafés with my cousins and their friends.

I'm having a great time here in India!

See you soon.

Nandeep

2 WRITING SKILLS
Correcting mistakes

a Correct the sentences.

1 I'm having a wonderful time here in france.
I'm having a wonderful time here in France.
2 Yesterday we visitted the Palace of Versailles near Paris.
______
3 In the mornings, I usually going to the beach with my Portuguese friends.
______
4 I hope your having a great time in Canada with your family.
______
5 Their English are very good, but we always speak in German.
______

3 WRITING

a Read the email from Paul. Use the notes in parentheses to write Maria's reply.

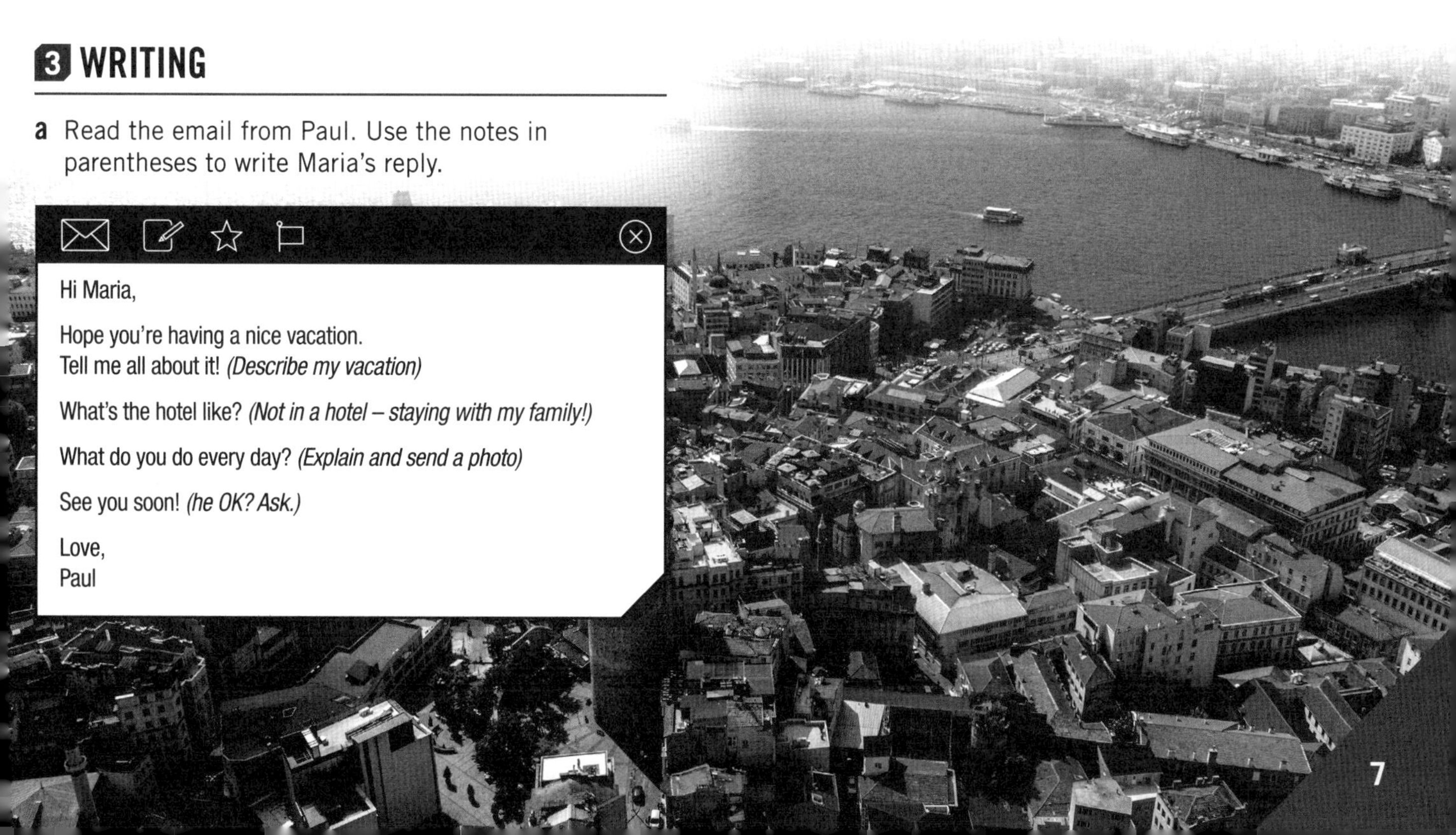

Hi Maria,

Hope you're having a nice vacation.
Tell me all about it! *(Describe my vacation)*

What's the hotel like? *(Not in a hotel – staying with my family!)*

What do you do every day? *(Explain and send a photo)*

See you soon! *(he OK? Ask.)*

Love,
Paul

UNIT 1

Reading and listening extension

1 READING

a Read the article. Match the statements 1–3 with the people a–c.

1 Living abroad is different from living in the U.S. — b
2 Not everyone would love working abroad.
3 It's important to see new places often.

a Vanessa
b Juan
c Emma

WORKING ABROAD: **IS IT FOR YOU?**

Are you looking for a new challenge at work? Do you want to meet new people and travel? A lot of people work abroad to experience a new culture. Americans especially have a positive experience — 74% of Americans who live abroad say they feel at home in their new country! I talked to some young people from the U.S. about their experiences.

EMMA, 27, MEXICO CITY

I work as an English teacher in Mexico City. It's an amazing city! It's cheap to live here, so I'm saving a lot of money. Working abroad is not for everyone. I love Mexico, but I miss home, too. My plan is to return home in three months. One year abroad is enough for me!

VANESSA, 25, SÃO PAULO

I've been in São Paulo for two years. I work in IT. My job is sometimes boring, but the city is exciting! I've also traveled to other parts of the country. It's cheap to travel in Brazil, so I try to see a new city or town once a month. I'd like to stay here for a long time and never stop seeing new places.

JUAN, 24, PARIS

Living in Paris is very different from back home, but I love my life here. I'm studying basic French and working as an event planner for an American company. I travel all over Europe for work and have friends and coworkers in many countries — my life is very exciting!

There might be some difficulties with living abroad, but a lot of people are doing it these days. It helps you grow professionally and personally. Why don't you see what opportunities are outside your country?

b Read the article again and check (✓) the best endings for the sentences.

1 Americans living abroad …
   a ☐ rarely feel comfortable in their new countries.
   b ☑ often have a positive experience.
   c ☐ always want to return home after a year.
2 Emma …
   a ☐ has been in Mexico three months.
   b ☐ thinks Mexico City is wonderful.
   c ☐ wants to stay abroad more than a year.
3 Vanessa …
   a ☐ thinks that São Paulo is a cheap city.
   b ☐ thinks her job is exciting.
   c ☐ often travels outside of São Paulo.
4 Juan …
   a ☐ doesn't speak a lot of French.
   b ☐ works with only Americans.
   c ☐ travels to the U.S. for work.
5 The writer of the article thinks that …
   a ☐ living abroad is easy.
   b ☐ living abroad can help you with future jobs.
   c ☐ there are many opportunities to work abroad.

c Write a paragraph about the good and bad parts of living and working abroad. Think about:

- family and friends
- some problems with the new language and culture
- the stories on the website
- your own experience.

2 LISTENING

a 01.06 Listen to the podcast. Match 1–3 with a–c to make true sentences.

1 Sophia — a sees people from a school club every week.
2 Carson — b is friends with the people he lives with.
3 Luis — c meets people in a café every week.

b 01.06 Listen to the podcast again and check (✓) the best endings for the sentences.

1 The podcast is about …
- a ☐ starting college.
- b ☐ moving to a new city.
- c ✓ how people make friends.

2 Carson doesn't …
- a ☐ usually go out at night.
- b ☐ like making friends with new people.
- c ☐ find it difficult to meet people at college.

3 Carson likes …
- a ☐ going to parties with his friends.
- b ☐ people who like similar things to him.
- c ☐ the nature near where he lives.

4 Sophia is interested in …
- a ☐ making friends with people studying acting.
- b ☐ joining a club.
- c ☐ meeting a lot of different people.

5 Luis doesn't …
- a ☐ use the Internet to meet people.
- b ☐ like the people he lives with.
- c ☐ usually go out at night.

6 Which of the sentences is true about the students?
- a ☐ The college is helping all the students make friends.
- b ☐ The students are making friends in different ways.

c Write questions and answers about what you do in your free time and who you spend it with. Think about these questions:

- Where do you spend your free time?
- What do you do and how often?
- Who do you spend your free time with?

Review and extension

1 GRAMMAR

Correct the sentences.

1 Where you went on vacation last year?
Where did you go on vacation last year?
2 At the moment, she works at the café by the bus station.
3 Why you missed the bus?
4 I can't talk to you now because I do my homework.
5 What kind of music you usually listen to?
6 They waiting for the bus to Dallas.

2 VOCABULARY

Correct the sentences.

1 The new Batman movie is amaizing!
The new Batman movie is amazing!
2 We very enjoyed the movie last night.
3 We had a wonderfull time at the party last night.
4 I think our Italian class is so borring.
5 I think that man's a little extrange. Look, he's talking to himself.
6 New York's allright, but I prefer to live in Los Angeles.

3 WORDPOWER *like*

Match 1–8 with a–h to make sentences.

1 [*e*] We can go for a walk in the park
2 ☐ What was the party
3 ☐ What amazing weather! It looks
4 ☐ The boy in the white T-shirt looks
5 ☐ He loves movies with superheroes, you know,
6 ☐ I absolutely love this singer. She sounds
7 ☐ I want to buy a computer
8 ☐ Thanks for your email. It sounds

a like the perfect day for the beach.
b like this one. How much is it?
c like Jacob. They have the same smile.
d like you're having a great vacation.
e if you like.
f like Katy Perry.
g like Batman or Spider-Man.
h like last night?

REVIEW YOUR PROGRESS

Look again at Review Your Progress on p. 16 of the Student's Book. How well can you do these things now?
3 = very well 2 = well 1 = not so well

I CAN …	
ask and answer personal questions	☐
talk about how I communicate	☐
greet people and end conversations	☐
write a personal email.	☐

2A WE HAD AN ADVENTURE

1 GRAMMAR Simple past

a Check (✓) the correct sentences. Correct the wrong sentences.

1 ☐ The train not arrived until 10:30 p.m., so we got home around midnight.
The train didn't arrive until 10:30 p.m., so we got home around midnight.

2 ☐ I slept very badly on the plane, so I feeled very tired the next day.
____

3 ☐ Did you took the train from New York to Washington?
____

4 ☐ We flew from Chicago to Detroit because it was really cheap.
____

5 ☐ They spended two nights at a hotel, and then they stayed at a friend's house for three days.
____

6 ☐ I didn't enjoyed my trip to New Orleans because the weather wasn't very good.
____

7 ☐ When I got back to my hotel, I got a text from my sister.
____

8 ☐ We unpacked our suitcases and ate dinner at the hotel restaurant. It cost 100 dollars!
____

b Complete the exchanges with the simple past form of the verbs in parentheses. Use contractions where possible.

1 **A** How *was* (be) your flight?
B Fine, thanks, but I ____________ (not sleep) because the seats ____________ (not be) comfortable.

2 **A** What ____________ (you, do) last summer?
B We ____________ (not have) much money, so we ____________ (decide) to stay in Florida.

3 **A** Where ____________ (Ben, go) on vacation last year?
B He ____________ (go) to Canada.

4 **A** ____________ (you, bring) back any souvenirs from Jamaica?
B Yes, I ____________. (do) I ____________ (buy) some Blue Mountain coffee.

5 **A** ____________ (you, see) your French friends when you were in Paris?
B Yes, we ____________. (do) We ____________ (meet) them for dinner one evening.

6 **A** ____________ (you, visit) your cousins in Los Angeles?
B No, we ____________ (not have) time.

2 VOCABULARY Tourism

a Match 1–8 with a–h to make sentences.

1 [d] We decided to go to China on vacation, so we had to get
2 ☐ I'm really bored. Why don't we do
3 ☐ James decided to go away
4 ☐ Going to the Olympics is great, but you need to book
5 ☐ It's a good idea to buy
6 ☐ Come on! Let's unpack
7 ☐ My daughter didn't have a lot of money, so she stayed
8 ☐ On the day you leave, you need to check out of

a to Mexico for the weekend.
b our suitcases and go out for lunch.
c in hostels when she went traveling for a year.
d a visa from the embassy.
e some sightseeing this afternoon?
f your accommodation before you go.
g your hotel by 11 o'clock.
h souvenirs here – they're very expensive at the airport.

b Write the names of the vacation items under the pictures.

1 *sunscreen*

2 ____________

3 ____________

4 ____________

5 ____________

6 ____________

3 PRONUNCIATION *-ed* endings

a Check (✓) the verbs that have an extra syllable when we add *-ed*.

Infinitive	+ *-ed*	Extra syllable?
depart	departed	✓
love	loved	
listen	listened	
hate	hated	
sound	sounded	
look	looked	
post	posted	
invite	invited	
enjoy	enjoyed	
like	liked	

b ▶ 02.01 Listen and check.

2B EVERYONE WAS WAITING FOR ME

1 VOCABULARY Travel collocations

a Complete the sentences with the correct forms of the verbs in the box.

miss take off get to change give
land leave for board ~~travel around~~

When I was a student, my best friend and I [1]<u>*traveled around*</u> Europe for a month. We rented a car and [2]__________ other travelers a ride with a ride-sharing app. It was a great way to save money and meet people!

She [3]__________ her vacation at six o'clock in the morning. However, she [4]__________ the 6:30 train because there was a traffic jam downtown.

Our plane [5]__________ from Beijing 45 minutes late, but we [6]__________ in Sydney 10 minutes early!

Our trip from Washington, D.C. to New York was terrible! We [7]__________ our train in Washington, D.C. at two o'clock, but then we [8]__________ trains in Baltimore and also in Philadelphia. In the end, we [9]__________ New York just after midnight!

b <u>Underline</u> the correct words to complete the sentences.

1 **A** Why was there a big *strike* / <u>*traffic jam*</u> / *ride* on the highway this morning?
  B Because there was a two-car *crash* / *strike* / *line* at 7:30.
2 **A** Why did you *lose* / *miss* / *delay* your train?
  B Well, my friend was driving us to the station, but her GPS gave us the wrong directions, so we *left* / *broke down* / *got lost*. In the end, we asked someone for help!
3 **A** Why were there *traffic jams* / *long delays* / *long lines* for all the flights from Heathrow Airport today?
  B Because there was a pilots' *strike* / *turbulence* / *delay* yesterday, so a lot of planes are at the wrong airport today.
4 There was *a turbulence* / *something wrong* / *a strike* with our bus, so we waited for two hours at the bus station.
5 It took me over an hour to get my ticket because there was a long *delay* / *line* / *crash* at the ticket office. Then the train *got lost* / *took off* / *broke down* just outside Paris, so that's why I'm so late.
6 **A** It sounds like you had a bad flight between Washington and London.
  B Yes, there was a lot of *turbulence* / *lines* / *strikes* over the Atlantic because of the bad weather.

2 GRAMMAR Past continuous

a Complete the sentences with the past continuous forms of the verbs in parentheses.

1 When we arrived at the bus station, my uncle <u>*was waiting*</u> for us in the parking lot. (wait)
2 It __________ hard when we got to our hotel. (snow)
3 __________ over the Andes when the turbulence started? (you, fly)
4 How fast __________ when the accident happened? (you, drive)
5 Where __________ when the thief stole your bag? (you, stand)
6 Did you get lost because your phone __________? (not work)

b Complete the text with the simple past or past continuous forms of the verbs in parentheses.

My mother and I [1]<u>*had*</u> (have) a terrible trip from Portland to Seattle last weekend. First, when my brother [2]__________ (drive) us to the airport on Saturday evening, his car [3]__________ (break down) on the highway. In the end, we [4]__________ (miss) our plane and [5]__________ (buy) some new tickets for the flight on Sunday morning instead. However, on Sunday morning we [6]__________(wait) for our flight when it [7]__________ (start) snowing heavily, and they [8]__________ (decide) to close the airport. So we [9]__________ (take) a taxi to the train station and [10]__________ (buy) tickets for the 2 p.m. train to Seattle.

3 PRONUNCIATION Vowel sounds

a 02.02 Listen to the sentences. Do the letters in **bold** sound like /ʌ/ as in *up* or /ɜ/ as in *her*? Check (✓) the correct box for each sentence.

	/ʌ/ (e.g., **u**p)	/ɜ/ (e.g., h**er**)
1 W**er**e you waiting for the bus?		✓
2 I w**a**sn't driving the car.		
3 They w**er**e watching TV.		
4 We w**er**en't having dinner.		
5 She w**a**s talking on her phone.		
6 W**a**s she listening?		
7 He w**a**sn't smoking.		
8 They w**er**en't playing chess.		

2C EVERYDAY ENGLISH
What time's the next train?

1 USEFUL LANGUAGE
Asking for information in a public place

a Put the words in the correct order to make questions.

1 anything else / help you / with / I / there / is / can ?
Is there anything else I can help you with?
2 is / tell / where / information desk / you / me / the / could ?
____
3 Boston / to / much / is / a round-trip ticket / how ?
____
4 for the airport / leave / do / often / buses / how / the ?
____
5 Barcelona / time / the next train / what / to / is ?
____
6 my ticket / pay / dollars / can / for / in / I ?
____
7 can / a sandwich / the trip / for / where / buy / I ?
____
8 a taxi / to the airport / much / it / does / cost / to get / how ?
____

b 02.03 Listen and check.

c Complete the conversation with the words in the box.

can near here have over there could you ~~excuse~~ anything else actually from what time

A [1] Excuse me.
B Yes, how [2]________ I help you?
A [3]________ tell me which platform the next train to Chicago leaves [4]________?
B Of course. It leaves from platform 2.
A OK, thanks. And [5]________ does it leave?
B It leaves at 10:32, in 12 minutes.
A Great. Thanks.
B Is there [6]________ I can help you with?
A [7]________, there is one more thing. Where can I buy some coffee? Is there a café [8]________ ?
B Yes, there is. There's a café on the platform, [9]________.
A Great. Thanks so much.
B No problem. [10]________ a good trip.

d 02.04 Listen and check.

e Match the traveler's sentences 1–8 with the attendant's responses a–h.

1 [c] Hello.
2 [ ] Could you tell me what time the next bus to Atlanta leaves, please?
3 [ ] Great, thanks! And where does it leave from?
4 [ ] I will be. Can I have a ticket, please?
5 [ ] Here you are. Also, is there somewhere I can buy a bottle of water?
6 [ ] That's OK. I can run fast.
7 [ ] Yes, I think that's it. Thank you for your help!
8 [ ] Thanks! Bye!

a Goodbye!
b Yes, of course. It leaves in five minutes.
c Good afternoon. How can I help you?
d Sure. That'll be $9.50.
e No problem, sir. Now hurry, or you'll miss your bus!
f From gate number 4, but you'll need to be quick!
g You'll need to! Is that all, sir?
h Yes, at the newsstand over there, but I'm not sure you'll have time.

2 PRONUNCIATION Connecting words

a 02.05 Listen to the questions. Check (✓) the two words that are joined together.

1 When did you check into your hotel?
a [✓] **check** into b [ ] your **h**otel
2 How can I help you?
a [ ] ca**n I** b [ ] hel**p y**ou
3 Did you get a visa when you went to China?
a [ ] ge**t a** b [ ] whe**n y**ou
4 What time did your plane take off?
a [ ] di**d y**our b [ ] ta**ke o**ff
5 What time is your train?
a [ ] ti**me i**s b [ ] i**s y**our
6 How much is a round-trip ticket to Bogotá?
a [ ] mu**ch i**s b [ ] t**o B**ogotá

2D SKILLS FOR WRITING
This city is different, but very friendly

1 READING

a Read Roberto's blog and check (✓) the correct answers.

1 Roberto and Ana are staying in …
  - a ☐ a hotel in downtown London.
  - b ☐ a hostel near Heathrow Airport.
  - c ☐ a hotel in Earl's Court.
  - d ☐ a hostel near downtown London.

2 On Sunday, Roberto and Ana …
  - a ☐ had fish and chips for lunch.
  - b ☐ spent all day at the British Museum.
  - c ☐ went to the British Museum and Covent Garden.
  - d ☐ thought the British Museum was boring.

SATURDAY

Ana and I got to London at 11:30 this morning. It was a very long flight from São Paulo. When we got off the plane, the first thing we noticed was the cold – six degrees! I'm glad I brought a warm coat! In São Paulo, it was 35 degrees when we left. Everything they say about Londoners is true! The people at the airport weren't very friendly, and they couldn't understand our English. And we couldn't understand what they were saying. In the end, we took the subway from Heathrow Airport to our hostel in Earl's Court, near downtown London. The hostel is full of young tourists from all over the world, and everyone was very friendly and helpful. We were very tired, so we decided to sleep for a few hours. Ana's telling me to get ready to go and eat, so I have to finish now – more tomorrow.

SUNDAY

Ana and I had our first experience of British food last night. We went to a little café near the hostel. We decided to try fish and chips. It's a typical British dish and it was delicious with a hot cup of tea (with milk!). Today we visited the British Museum and Covent Garden. The British Museum is amazing – there are lots of interesting things to see. We spent two hours there and only saw a few of the rooms. We bought some sandwiches for lunch, and then we went to Covent Garden market. There were lots of musicians and magicians in the street. We had a great afternoon, and Ana took a lot of photos. You can see them on Facebook.

b Read the blog again. Are the sentences true or false?

1 On Saturday, it was warmer in London than in São Paulo.
2 It was difficult for Roberto and Ana to understand the people at the airport.
3 When they got to the hostel, they went to bed.
4 They didn't enjoy their fish and chips.
5 They didn't see all the rooms in the British Museum.
6 They had lunch in a restaurant in Covent Garden.

2 WRITING SKILLS Linking words

a Underline the correct words to complete the sentences.

1 There was a long line for the museum, *and* / <u>*so*</u> / *but* we decided to go to the market instead.
2 We didn't visit the Tower of London *because* / *so* / *but* the tickets were very expensive.
3 The hotel looked really nice, *because* / *and* / *but* they didn't have any free rooms that night.
4 Yesterday I visited Ellis Island *so* / *and* / *because* the Statue of Liberty.
5 There weren't any flights today *but* / *so* / *because* there was a snowstorm.
6 *Because* / *When* / *So* we got to our hotel, I called my wife to wish her a happy birthday.
7 It started raining hard, *but* / *because* / *so* we didn't go to the mountains.
8 We wanted to go to the concert, *but* / *so* / *because* we couldn't get any tickets.

3 WRITING

a Read the notes. Write Maite's blog post about her vacation in New York.

Maite's blog: New York post (notes)

<u>Monday, January 25</u>

Quito: left 12:20 p.m.
New York: arrived 10:30 p.m.
Very tired – (why?)
Weather: very cold – minus 6 degrees!
People = (?)
Hotel = (?)
Dinner = (?)

UNIT 2
Reading and listening extension

1 READING

a Read the article. How did the couples travel? Check (✓) the correct ways. Sometimes there is more than one possible answer.

1 Ben and Sam
   a ☐ on foot
   b ☑ on two wheels
   c ☑ on four wheels
   d ☐ by boat
2 Beto and Katie
   a ☐ on foot
   b ☐ on two wheels
   c ☐ on four wheels
   d ☐ by boat
3 Aika and Rob
   a ☐ on foot
   b ☐ on two wheels
   c ☐ on four wheels
   d ☐ by boat

b Read the article again and underline the correct words to complete the sentences.

1 *Ben and Sam / Beto and Katie / Aika and Rob* stayed in San Diego for most of the week.
2 *Ben and Sam / Beto and Katie / Aika and Rob* enjoyed the first day of the race.
3 *Ben and Sam / Beto and Katie / Aika and Rob* stopped when they didn't know where they were.
4 *Ben and Sam / Beto and Katie / Aika and Rob* finished their trip on foot when something happened to the vehicle they were in.
5 *Ben and Sam / Beto and Katie / Aika and Rob* stopped after the first day.

c Complete the words to make sentences about the article. Write one word in each space.

1 During the race, the students c<u>ouldn't</u>______ spend any money.
2 When they started the race, the weather was s____________.
3 Ben and Sam got a r____________ home with Ben's dad.
4 It c____________ money for Beto and Katie to stay at a hotel.
5 Aika and Rob got to Mexico late in the a____________.

d Write about a long trip you went on. Remember to include:

- where you went
- a description of how you traveled there
- what you thought of the place.

In July, a group of students from San Diego State University, in California, had a race. It started at the university at 9 a.m. on June 20. The winners were the pair who traveled the longest distance in seven days without spending any money.

BEN AND SAM

We decided to bike. The sun was shining when we left, and it was fun. But on the third day, it started raining and we got lost. It was awful. We slept under a tree in a field. The next morning, Ben called his dad, and he came to get us and drove us home.

Distance traveled: 110 miles

BETO AND KATIE

A friend gave us a ride on her way to her parents' house, but there were long delays and we didn't go far for hours. That evening as we were driving north, her car broke down, and we had to get out. We didn't know what to do. We were tired and hungry, so we decided to walk to a small town and stay at a hotel. But we had to pay. The next day, we went home.

Distance traveled: 130 miles

AIKA AND ROB

We decided to walk to the port in San Diego and try to board a ship. We went to the office and asked if any ships would take us for free. For five days no one would. On the sixth day, we found a ship to take us to Mexico. We boarded the ship and ten hours later, we arrived in Mexico as the sun was setting. It was amazing.

Distance traveled: 75 miles

2 LISTENING

a 02.06 Listen to the conversation. Match problems a–e with where they are happening 1–5.

1 85 ______________	a crash and delays
2 75	b long delays
3 20	c no delays
4 Subways	d problems this weekend
5 Hartsfield-Jackson	e traffic jam

b 02.06 Listen to the conversation again and check (✓) the correct answers.

1 Why were there delays on 85 this morning?
 a ☑ There was a crash.
 b ☐ The police closed the road.
 c ☐ It was raining.

2 What happened three hours ago near Hapeville?
 a ☐ There was an accident.
 b ☐ There was a very long line of cars
 c ☐ A truck stopped working.

3 Who should use Metropolitan Parkway this evening?
 a ☐ people who are going to Hapeville
 b ☐ trucks
 c ☐ everyone on 75

4 Who did the police say can't walk on the side of the highway?
 a ☐ people going to the annual fall festival
 b ☐ people flying from the airport
 c ☐ people who want to camp

5 What is unusual about the subway today?
 a ☐ There aren't any subway lines working.
 b ☐ The subway lines are working well.
 c ☐ There are lots of delays.

6 Where did James and Fatima stay last night?
 a ☐ at a hotel by the airport
 b ☐ on the floor at the airport
 c ☐ in India

c Write about a long trip you took. Remember to include:

- how you traveled
- how long it took
- what problems you had.

Review and extension

1 GRAMMAR

Correct the sentences.

1 When I did some housework, I heard the news on the radio.
When I was doing some housework, I heard the news on the radio.
2 When we were getting to the station, the train was just arriving.
3 My wife called me while I waited for my plane.
4 A man was taking my wallet while I was waiting in line for my ticket.
5 Last year, we were going on vacation to Costa Rica for two weeks.
6 I was driving to the airport when I was seeing the accident.

2 VOCABULARY

Correct the sentences.

1 They missed their flight because Rob's car broke on the way to the airport.
They missed their flight because Rob's car broke down on the way to the airport.
2 My travel from Miami to Memphis took 15 hours.
3 Last week, I went to Rome on a business travel.
4 The trafic was terrible because it was the rush hour.
5 By the time they checked away the hotel, it was 2 p.m.
6 In the afternoon, they went sighsee in the old town.

3 WORDPOWER *off*

Complete the sentences with the words in the box.

75% I'm cut ~~turned~~ drove took are fell

1 He was tired when he went to bed, so he *turned* off the light and went to sleep.
2 Paul ______________ off a piece of bread for me so I could try it.
3 When I got to the hotel, I ______________ off my shoes.
4 She ______________ off her motorcycle and broke her arm.
5 Those jeans are cheap! They're ______________ off the original price.
6 He got in his car and ______________ off without speaking.
7 Good night. ______________ off now. I'm meeting a friend.
8 Ladies and gentlemen: the movie is about to start, so please make sure your phones ______________ off.

REVIEW YOUR PROGRESS

Look again at Review Your Progress on p. 26 of the Student's Book. How well can you do these things now?
3 = very well 2 = well 1 = not so well

I CAN ...	
talk about past vacations	☐
describe travel problems	☐
ask for information in a public place	☐
write a travel blog.	☐

3A I'VE NEVER SEEN CROWDS LIKE THIS

1 GRAMMAR
Present perfect or simple past

a Put the words in the correct order to make sentences.

1 for / has / that old woman / gone / grocery shopping / James / a lot of times .
James has gone grocery shopping for that old woman a lot of times.

2 you / have / to / been / in / Rio de Janeiro / carnival / ever ?
____

3 and cell phone / I / TV / a new / bought / this month .
____

4 have / you / from / borrowed / money / me / never .
____

5 they / volunteer work / ever / done / have / any ?
____

6 big / never / a / for a server / left / tip / has / she .
____

7 money / have / any / you / homeless person / to / given / ever / a ?
____

8 several / I / found / this month / good bargains .
____

b Complete the exchanges with the present perfect or simple past forms of the words in parentheses.

1 **A** Have you ever given money to charity? (you, ever, give)
B Yes, I __________ $10 to a cancer charity last week. (give)

2 **A** __________ for a discount at a store before? (she, ever, ask)
B Yes, she __________ for a discount on some shoes, and they offered her 10% off! (ask)

3 **A** __________ someone who was hurt? (you, ever, help)
B Yes, I __________ a woman who fell off her bike last week. (help)

4 **A** I __________ tips in that restaurant lots of times. (leave)
B Really? How much __________ the last time you went? (you, leave)

5 **A** __________ something online? (he, ever, buy)
B Yes, he __________ a new jacket that was on sale last month. (buy)

2 VOCABULARY
Money and shopping

a Match 1–8 with a–h to make sentences.

1 [f] I follow my favorite stores on Facebook
2 [ ] That vacation sounds fantastic, but
3 [ ] My brother lent me $50 yesterday
4 [ ] If you can't afford to buy a new car,
5 [ ] She just spent $150
6 [ ] I only buy clothes from that store
7 [ ] If you buy two jackets,
8 [ ] When I borrow money

a so I could buy some new jeans.
b from my parents, I always pay it back quickly.
c when they have special offers.
d we can offer you a 20% discount.
e on two pairs of shoes.
f so I know when they have a sale.
g it costs $3,000 for just a week!
h why don't you get a loan from the bank?

b Complete the text with the words in the box.

into	afford	lend	spend	bank account
~~up for~~	borrow	back	loan	

I'm saving [1] up for a car at the moment. I put $200 [2]__________ my [3]__________ every month. I can't [4]__________ to buy a new car, so it will have to be second-hand – probably three or four years old. My parents have offered to [5]__________ me some money, but I don't want to [6]__________ any money from them. They've just bought a very old house in the country, and they need to [7]__________ a lot of money on repairs. So I'm going to ask the bank for a [8]__________ of $5,000. I think I can pay it [9]__________ in two years.

3B I'VE ALREADY GIVEN $25 TO CHARITY

1 VOCABULARY
make / do / give collocations

a Match 1–8 with a–h to make sentences.

1 [d] She was very confident, so she made
2 [ ] When she read the email from her nephew, it made
3 [ ] Are you doing anything
4 [ ] He's a really funny guy. He always makes
5 [ ] Your daughter's very smart. Is she doing
6 [ ] My grandfather always gives us
7 [ ] We gave the tourists
8 [ ] He didn't use his camera anymore, so he gave it

a away to his grandson.
b silly jokes when he's with friends.
c a big hug when we go to see him.
d a lot of friends at her new school.
e fun for your birthday?
f directions to the train station.
g well in school this year?
h her smile because it was so funny.

b Underline the correct words to complete the sentences.

1 I love those old black-and-white movies. Charlie Chaplin always *does* / *makes* / *gives* me smile.
2 You're so rude. You never *do* / *make* / *give* the servers a tip.
3 He *made* / *did* / *gave* volunteer work for a charity in Africa last year.
4 She was so happy to see him again that she *gave* / *made* / *did* him a big hug.
5 Do your parents usually *make* / *give* / *do* something nice for their wedding anniversary?
6 I'm having a great time in Panama City. I've *made* / *done* / *given* some new friends at the hostel.
7 The doctors say that she's *making* / *giving* / *doing* well and that she can leave the hospital tomorrow.
8 I've never *made* / *given* / *done* anyone directions in Spanish – all the tourists who come here speak English.

2 GRAMMAR
Present perfect with *already* and *yet*

a Underline the correct adverbs to complete the sentences.

1 Has she helped her sister with her homework *yet* / *already*?
2 Have you *already* / *yet* visited your grandmother this week?
3 He's *already* / *yet* done a great job, and it's only his second week with the company!
4 We haven't given away our old clothes *already* / *yet*.
5 Thanks for the invitation, but we've *already* / *yet* eaten dinner.
6 I haven't given her any advice *yet* / *already*, but I will if she asks me.
7 We haven't done that task *yet* / *already*. We need more time.
8 She's *already* / *yet* made a list of the things she needs.

b Correct the sentences.

1 Mike hasn't yet gone shopping.
Mike hasn't gone shopping yet.
2 He's made already a payment of $2,000.
____
3 Have you yet given your parents directions?
____
4 Eva already has given good advice.
____
5 I haven't made yet any new friends at school.
____
6 Has she done yet any volunteer work?
____
7 I've bought already a present for my wife.
____
8 Already they've given $1,000 away to charity.
____

3C EVERYDAY ENGLISH

Do you have anything cheaper?

1 USEFUL LANGUAGE Talking to people in stores

a Put the conversation in the correct order.

- ☐ **B** Mm, I think she'd like them. On second thought, maybe I should get something else.
- 1 **A** Good morning. Can I help you?
- ☐ **B** Do you have anything cheaper?
- ☐ **A** OK. Um, let me see … what about this necklace?
- ☐ **B** Yes, it's beautiful. OK, I'll take it.
- ☐ **A** Are you looking for anything in particular?
- ☐ **B** Um, yes. I'm looking for a present for my mother.
- ☐ **A** Really? How about these earrings? They're really beautiful. A perfect present …
- ☐ **B** Well, she loves earrings.
- ☐ **A** Well, these earrings here are cheaper. They're only $30 with the discount.

b 03.01 Listen and check.

c <u>Underline</u> the correct words to complete the sentences.

1. How would you like to *cost* / <u>*pay*</u> / *buy*?
2. We're looking *for* / *at* / *after* a present for my grandfather.
3. Did you want something *on* / *in* / *at* particular?
4. Who's *then* / *after* / *next*, please?
5. *In second thought* / *On second thought* / *My second thought*, I really think we should get her a book.
6. Can you *enter* / *write* / *touch* your PIN, please?
7. Do you have this in a different *size* / *register* / *receipt*? Thanks.
8. Could you show us *something more* / *something else* / *something other*?

d Put the words in the correct order to make sentences.

1. for / jacket / looking / a / I'm .
   I'm looking for a jacket.
2. a / 14 / size / I'm / I / think .
   ______
3. same / in / have / one / blue / do / the / you ?
   ______
4. much / tell / can / it / how / is / you / me ?
   ______
5. a little / too / that's / expensive .
   ______
6. one / you / cheaper / do / have / a ?
   ______

2 PRONUNCIATION Sentence stress

a 03.02 Listen to the sentences and <u>underline</u> the stressed syllables or words.

1. Can you <u>show</u> us something <u>else</u>?
2. Can you enter your PIN, please?
3. I'm looking for a present for my husband.
4. Do you have any black jeans?
5. Thanks. I'll take it.
6. Actually, I think we should buy her a book.

3D SKILLS FOR WRITING
We've successfully raised $500

1 READING

a Read David and Philip's email and check (✓) the correct answer.

David and Philip are writing to …

a ☐ ask their coworkers for more money.
b ☐ invite their coworkers to a party.
c ☐ tell their coworkers about Cancer Research and how they have all helped.
d ☐ ask their coworkers to swim a mile.

b Read David and Philip's email again. Are the sentences true or false?

1 In the last year, they have given $2,500 to Cancer Research.
2 In April, 30 people swam a mile to raise money.
3 The party in June was very popular.
4 Four thousand people with cancer get money from Cancer Research.

Hello everyone,

We'd like to say a big "Thank you!" to everyone who has helped us raise money for Cancer Research over the past six months. We've successfully raised $2,500!

We really hope you have enjoyed the different events that we have organized this year. First, we had a "Swimathon" in April. Thirty of us swam a mile and raised over $1,000. Then 200 people came to our fantastic summer party in June. And don't forget to come to our special quiz night in September. There are some amazing prizes!

Cancer Research will use the money to do important research. This includes the work of over 4,000 scientists, doctors, and nurses who are fighting cancer in this country. Cancer Research helps thousands of people with cancer every year.

Would you like to help us raise more money for Cancer Research? Please look out for the next event. Thanks again for all your help.

David and Philip

2 WRITING SKILLS Paragraphing

a Read the sentences. Put them in the correct order to make an email with four paragraphs. The paragraphs should be in the following order:

- Introduction
- How the team has raised / raises money
- Information about ActionAid
- Closing the email

☐ Thanks again for all your help. Please look out for our next event.
☐ ActionAid will use the money to help poor people around the world, to educate them, and to protect them. In the past ten years, they have helped thousands of children start school.
☐ We have successfully raised $750.
☐ And, of course, next Friday there is the book and calendar sale at lunchtime.
1 We'd like to thank everyone for helping to raise money for ActionAid over the past year.
☐ Most of you came to the 1970s party in September. A lot of people also came to our karaoke night in November.
☐ So remember that a small amount of money can make a big difference. For example, only $4 per week gives a child in Africa clean water, education, and medicine.

3 WRITING

a Read the notes and write Sam's email to his coworkers about the Save the Children charity.

Email to coworkers about Save the Children

Introduction:
Thank you – everyone who helped raise money – past 12 months. How much?

How the team has raised money and future events:
September: sports day
October: 1990s karaoke night
Next week: quiz night + prizes!

Information about Save the Children:
Our money = save children's lives + better future
Last year STC helped 10m children around the world
Small amount of money = big difference, e.g., $3 saves lives of 8 children with a stomach virus

Closing the email
Help raise more money for STC?
Email me for info about future events
Thanks again

UNIT 3
Reading and listening extension

1 READING

a Read the magazine article. Complete the sentences with the numbers in the box.

100	12 million	13 million	~~138 million~~

1 A company bought the website for $ 138 million .
2 He started the website with $__________.
3 The website has more than __________ regular users.
4 Charities got $__________ from Martin after he sold the website.

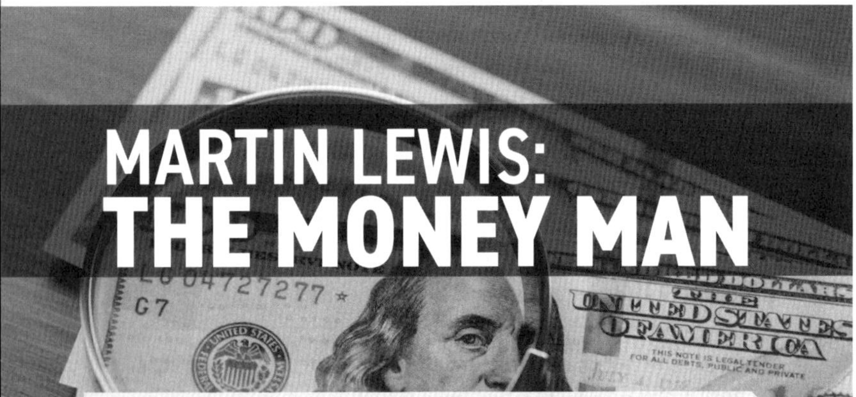

MARTIN LEWIS: THE MONEY MAN

Martin Lewis is a journalist, TV host, and writer. He knows a lot about money: how to spend it, where to use it, and most of all, how to save it!

Martin was always interested in saving money and helping other people save money. He gave tips to friends about it, he talked about it on television, and he wrote about it in a national newspaper. In 2003, he decided to start a website. He paid a man in Uzbekistan $100 to design the site, and soon thousands of people were using it. The website gave lots of useful information. It told people which times of the day supermarkets had the best offers. It helped people get discounts on everything from clothes to vacations. It told people when stores had sales. The website helped people buy things that they couldn't afford to buy before. And if you needed to borrow money to buy a new car or a house, it told you which banks were the best to lend it to you. A lot of people started using the site and started telling their friends about it.

The website has been a huge success, and Martin has done very well. Over 13 million people now use the site every month, and in 2012, Martin Lewis sold the site to another company for approximately $138 million. But Martin hasn't stopped helping people. Since selling the website, he has given away over $12 million to charities that help people look after their money. He's certainly made a lot of people smile. And it all started with $100.

b Read the magazine article again. Are the sentences true or false?

1 Martin Lewis is an expert on how to spend less money.
2 It took a long time before anyone used the website.
3 People can save money by going to supermarkets at a particular time of the day.
4 Martin Lewis still owns the website.
5 Martin's website made him a very rich man.

c Complete the summary of the magazine article with the correct forms of the verbs in the box.

borrow	buy	cost	get
save	spend	~~work~~	write

Before 2003, Martin Lewis [1] worked as a journalist and [2]__________ about how to save money. In 2003, it [3]__________ him $100 to start his website. Soon it was very popular. It has a lot of information about how to [4]__________ less money in stores, how to open a bank account, how to [5]__________ a discount on products, and where to [6]__________ money. The website has helped millions of people [7]__________ money or get a loan since 2003. A company [8]__________ the website in 2012 for $138 million.

d Write about something that you have borrowed from or lent to someone. Include answers to these questions:

- What was it?
- Who did you lend it to or borrow it from?
- For how long?

2 LISTENING

a 03.03 Listen to the conversation. Underline the correct people to complete the sentences.

1 *Anita / Gary / Mike* gave a man something that he didn't have.
2 *Anita / Gary / Mike* is helping a friend who doesn't have much money.
3 *Anita / Gary / Mike* does something nice for other people every week.
4 *Anita / Gary / Mike* asked other people to lend her things.
5 *Anita / Gary / Mike* made friends with the person he helped.

b 03.03 Listen to the conversation again and check (✓) the correct answers.

1 Why is Anita's neighbor having a party?
 a ☑ It's her daughter's birthday.
 b ☐ It's her son's birthday.
 c ☐ It's her husband's birthday.

2 Where is the birthday party going to be?
 a ☐ at the local beach
 b ☐ in the backyard
 c ☐ at the local park

3 What did the Colombian man do?
 a ☐ He borrowed an umbrella from Gary.
 b ☐ He lent an umbrella to Gary.
 c ☐ He borrowed Gary's jacket.

4 What happened when Gary saw the man again?
 a ☐ They had lunch.
 b ☐ They had coffee.
 c ☐ They went on vacation together.

5 What has Gary just bought?
 a ☐ a ticket to the theater
 b ☐ a ticket to Wilmington
 c ☐ a ticket to Colombia

6 How does Mike try to make people smile?
 a ☐ He gives them money.
 b ☐ He puts his arms around them.
 c ☐ He makes friends with them.

c Write about the nicest thing that you've ever done. Remember to include:

- who you helped
- why you helped them
- what you did
- how they felt and how you felt afterward.

Review and extension

1 GRAMMAR

Correct the sentences.

1 I never left a big tip in a restaurant.
 I've never left a big tip in a restaurant.
2 Did you ever give money to charity?
3 I've been to China on business last year.
4 I just bought a new cell phone.
5 I haven't bought yet a birthday present for my brother.
6 I already spent $200 this weekend.

2 VOCABULARY

Correct the sentences.

1 I've just opened an account bank in Ecuador.
 I've just opened a bank account in Ecuador.
2 Can you borrow me 50 dollars, please?
3 I don't have a card credit, so I always pay with cash.
4 James is saving on for a new computer.
5 Our taxi driver was very friendly, so we made him a big tip.
6 I bought a new laptop at sale – it was only $250!
7 Have you ever made any volunteer work?
8 Tony owes to me $50, but he hasn't paid me back yet.

3 WORDPOWER *just*

Complete the sentences with the words in the box.

about talked in time like ~~leaving~~ a beginner over under

1 I'm just *leaving*. I'll be there in ten minutes!
2 There was a lot of traffic, but we got to the airport just ________ for our flight.
3 My watch cost just ________ $100. Not cheap at all!
4 You're just ________ your mother – you have the same blue eyes!
5 Dinner is just ________ ready. It'll be five minutes.
6 The movie is 125 minutes long. It's just ________ two hours.
7 I just ________ to him. He'll meet us at 9:00.
8 No, she can't give a presentation in English yet. She's just ________.

REVIEW YOUR PROGRESS

Look again at Review Your Progress on p. 36 of the Student's Book. How well can you do these things now?
3 = very well 2 = well 1 = not so well

I CAN ...	
talk about money and shopping experiences	☐
talk about living with less	☐
talk to people in stores	☐
write an update email.	☐

4A I'M GOING TO THE HAIRDRESSER'S TOMORROW

1 VOCABULARY
Clothes and appearance

a Match the pictures with the words in the box.

underwear tights top tie high heels
tracksuit ~~gloves~~ sandals earrings sweater
flats bracelet

1 _gloves_

2 ___________

3 ___________

4 ___________

5 ___________

6 ___________

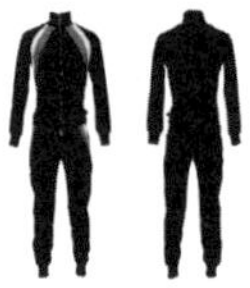
7 ___________

8 ___________

9 ___________

10 ___________

11 ___________

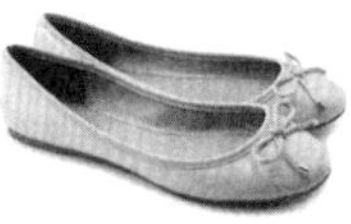
12 ___________

2 GRAMMAR
Present continuous and *be going to*

a Put the words in the correct order to make sentences.

1 buy / going / a new dress / I'm / the party / for / to .
I'm going to buy a new dress for the party.
2 going / your wedding / you / are / invite / your / to / cousin / to ?
____
3 not / going / they're / get married / to / this / year .
____
4 going / are / do / after college / you / what / to ?
____
5 visit / Spain next year / going / we're / in / my relatives / to .
____
6 to / you / are / wear / to / the party / what / going ?
____

b Complete the conversation with the present continuous forms of the verbs in the box. Use contractions where possible.

stay come bring not fly ~~arrive~~ take meet (x2)

A So what have you planned for this evening?
B Well, my parents [1] _are arriving_ at the station on the 5:30 train from Trenton.
A So, [2] ___________ you [3] ___________ them at the station?
B Yes, we are. We [4] ___________ a taxi from our house at 5:00.
A Good. So where [5] ___________ they [6] ___________?
B At the Hilton Hotel. They have a double room with a balcony.
A Great. And what about the restaurant?
B I've reserved a table for eight at seven o'clock. Everyone [7] ___________ to the restaurant at 6:45 so we can all be there when they arrive.
A Fantastic. Have you told the restaurant that it's your father's birthday?
B Yes, they've made him a special cake with HAPPY 60TH on it. They [8] ___________ it to our table at nine o'clock, together with the coffee.
A And what about tomorrow?
B They [9] ___________ to Chicago until the afternoon, so there's plenty of time. Their flight's at 3:30.
A Great, so it's all arranged. I have to go now because I [10] ___________ Sally for coffee in ten minutes. See you later!

c 04.01 Listen and check.

3 PRONUNCIATION
Sound and spelling: *going to*

a 04.02 Listen to *going to* in the sentences. Do you hear *going to* (/ˈgoʊ·ɪŋ tu/) or *gonna* (/ˌgɔ·nə/)? Check (✓) the correct box for each sentence.

	going to	*gonna*
1 Are you going to go out tonight?	☐	✓
2 What are you going to do for your birthday?	☐	☐
3 He's not going to take a vacation this year.	☐	☐
4 We're going to try to find a taxi.	☐	☐
5 I'm going to take a shower after breakfast.	☐	☐
6 They're not going to do their homework.	☐	☐
7 She's going to call her brother.	☐	☐
8 I'm not going to go to Cancún this year.	☐	☐

4B SHOULD WE GO TO THE MARKET?

1 GRAMMAR *will / won't / would / should*

a Match 1–8 with a–h to make sentences.

1 [c] Let's go to Greece on vacation next summer.
2 [ ] You know I don't really like spicy food.
3 [ ] What movie should we see with the kids?
4 [ ] Let's invite your parents for lunch next Sunday.
5 [ ] Hi. I'm at the supermarket, but I can't carry all the groceries on the bus. Would you pick me up?
6 [ ] Oh, no! We just missed the last bus.
7 [ ] Hi, Dad. I'm afraid I lost my cell phone.
8 [ ] Oh, no. I don't have enough money to buy this phone today.

a OK, should I call a taxi?
b Good idea. I'll call them later to see if they're free.
c Good idea. I'll check flights and hotel prices tomorrow.
d Don't worry. I'll buy you a new one for your birthday.
e Oh, that's too bad. Should I lend you some money?
f Don't worry. I'll bring the car and meet you there in ten minutes.
g Should we go see the new Disney movie?
h OK, we won't go to an Indian restaurant.

b <u>Underline</u> the correct words to complete the sentences.

1 **A** *Would* / <u>*Should*</u> / *Won't* we go to the movies tonight?
B Yes, OK. I *'ll* / *won't* / *should* check which movies are playing and call you back.
2 **A** Hi, Dad. I missed the last bus home!
B Don't worry. I *should* / *won't* / *'ll* bring the car and meet you by the movie theater.
3 What *will* / *should* / *won't* we do this weekend?
4 Don't worry. The station's very close to here, so you *'ll* / *would* / *won't* miss your bus.
5 **A** *Should* / *Will* / *Won't* we try to get tickets for the Imagine Dragons concert?
B Good idea. I *won't* / *should* / *'ll* check prices online.
6 I know you're a vegetarian, so I *would* / *won't* / *should* cook steak for dinner.
7 *Would* / *Won't* / *Should* you help me wash the dishes?
8 **A** Let's take Monica and Sara to that new Chinese restaurant for dinner.
B Yes, that's a great idea. *Would* / *Won't* / *Should* you call them and reserve a table for 7:30?

2 VOCABULARY Adjectives: places

a Complete the crossword puzzle.

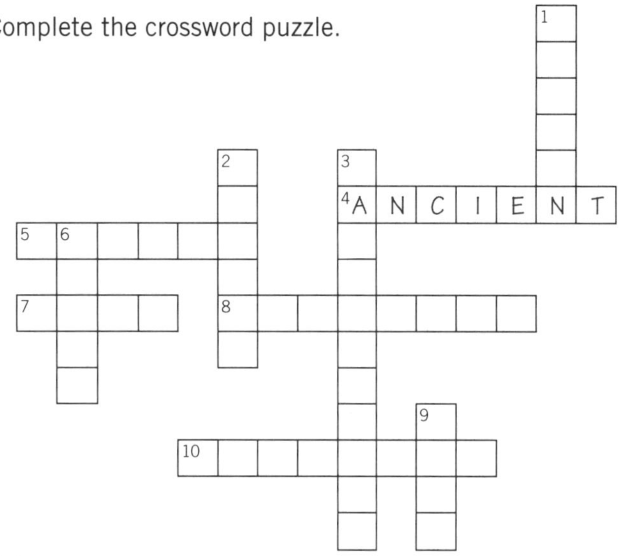

→ Across

4 Stonehenge is an <u>ancient</u> monument in Wiltshire in England. It's about 5,000 years old.
5 When the weather is really bad, we play on the i__________ tennis court at my local gym.
7 There are a lot of h__________ mountains in Switzerland. For example, the Matterhorn is about 4,500 meters above sea level.
8 I live in a very o__________ town. Nothing interesting happens here!
10 We live in a p__________ town. There's no traffic at all!

↓ Down

1 My school's in a really m__________ building. It's only five years old.
2 This road is very n__________. It isn't wide enough for a bus.
3 The view from the top of the Empire State Building is m__________.
6 It's very n__________ in this café, isn't it? It's difficult to hear you.
9 The British Museum is h__________. There are almost 600 rooms!

b Choose the opposites of the adjectives in **bold**. Use the words in the box.

modern	high	pretty	outdoor	quiet	~~wide~~

1 The streets in the old part of town are very **narrow**. <u>wide</u>
2 I think the new houses they've built are really **ugly**. __________
3 There is a big **indoor** swimming pool in my town. __________
4 That restaurant's always very **noisy**. __________
5 This is one of the most **ancient** cities in Greece. __________
6 The hills in New York are pretty **low**. __________

3 PRONUNCIATION Sound and spelling: *want* and *won't*

a 04.03 Listen and <u>underline</u> the correct words to complete the sentences.

1 We *won't* / <u>*want to*</u> go swimming today.
2 They *want to* / *won't* take you to the old mansion.
3 I *won't* / *want to* go to that restaurant again.
4 You *want to* / *won't* wait for the next bus.
5 I *won't* / *want to* study English again next year.
6 Felipe and I *want to* / *won't* invite him to our party.

4C EVERYDAY ENGLISH
Are you doing anything on Wednesday?

1 USEFUL LANGUAGE Making plans

a Put the conversation in the correct order.

- [ ] **A** Oh, OK. How about Friday? Is that OK for you?
- [ ] **B** Perfect!! Eleven o'clock. See you then.
- [ ] **A** OK, so you can't do this week. What are you doing next Monday?
- [ ] **B** Oh, that sounds nice. Let me check my phone. No, sorry, I can't do Wednesday. I'm going shopping with my mom.
- [1] **A** Are you doing anything on Wednesday? Would you like to get coffee?
- [ ] **B** Next Monday? Let me check. Nothing! I can do next Monday.
- [ ] **A** Great! So we can meet for coffee on Monday?
- [ ] **B** Friday … hang on a minute … no, sorry. I'm going to Seattle for the day. This week's really busy for me.
- [ ] **A** Should we meet at the Coffee Place at 11:00?
- [ ] **B** Yes, Monday's fine. Where should we go?

b 04.04 Listen and check.

c Put the words in the correct order to make sentences.

1 about / new / that / how / café / French ?
How about that new French café?
2 anything / doing / you / Saturday / this / are ?
______
3 busy / us / week's / really / this / for .
______
4 come / we / what / over / should / time ?
______
5 doing / next / you / Tuesday / are / what ?
______
6 over / you / come / would / for / to / lunch / like ?
______
7 can't / Thursday / I / this week / do .
______
8 for / Sunday / is / OK / you / this ?
______

d 04.05 Listen and check.

Ana's calendar

Sunday	a.m.	☆ day trip to Diablo Lake ☆
	lunch	
	p.m.	
Monday	a.m.	9–11 meeting at work
	lunch	1–2 lunch with Mom
	p.m.	
Tuesday	a.m.	7–9 aerobics class
	lunch	
	p.m.	6–8 movies with Kemal
Wednesday	a.m.	8–9 yoga
	lunch	
	p.m.	6:30 doctor's appointment
Thursday	a.m.	
	lunch	12–1 shopping with Karen
	p.m.	7–8:30 dance class
Friday	a.m.	
	lunch	all day – work conference
	p.m.	
Saturday	a.m.	
	lunch	day off!
	p.m.	

e Read Ana's calendar and underline the correct words to complete the telephone conversation.

SANDRA Hi, Ana! Are you free to meet on Monday morning?
ANA Let me check my calendar. I'm sorry, I have [1]*an aerobics class / a meeting / a doctor's appointment* then.
SANDRA Oh, that's too bad. How about Monday for lunch?
ANA No, I'm having lunch with [2]*Kemal / my mom / Karen* then.
SANDRA Oh, well ... are you doing anything on Tuesday evening?
ANA I'm afraid I'm going [3]*shopping / to the movies / to a dance class.*
SANDRA That sounds like fun! Let's see. I'm busy on Wednesday and Thursday. Could we meet on Friday?
ANA Unfortunately, I'm busy all day on Friday. I have a [4]*doctor's appointment / dance class / work conference.*
SANDRA OK. What are you doing this Sunday?
ANA Oh, dear. On Sunday I'm [5]*at a work conference / at Diablo Lake / in a meeting* all day.
SANDRA So you don't have any free time this week?
ANA Yes, I do! I have the whole day off on [6]*Wednesday / Thursday / Saturday*!

2 PRONUNCIATION Sentence stress

a 04.06 Listen to the sentences and underline the stressed words or syllables.

1 I can't meet you tomorrow.
2 He can meet us at the station.
3 I didn't understand him.
4 She hasn't seen that movie.
5 I have to start cooking dinner.
6 They don't like basketball.

4D SKILLS FOR WRITING
Are you free on Saturday?

1 READING

a Read Abby's email to Tony and his reply, and check (✓) the correct answer.

a ☐ Abby invites Tony and Laura to come to a birthday party at her house.
b ☐ Abby and Mike would like to go to a Chinese restaurant with Tony and Laura.
c ☐ Abby wants to see Tony and Laura's new house.
d ☐ Abby invites Tony and Laura to celebrate Mike's birthday at a Chinese restaurant.

Hi Tony,

How are things? We haven't seen you in ages. I hope you and Laura are well and enjoying your new house.

Are you doing anything on Friday, June 21? It's Mike's 40th birthday, and we're going to our favorite Chinese restaurant, Xian, with some friends. We're going to reserve a table for eight o'clock. Can you come? It would be great to see you both and have a chance to talk.

Everyone's bringing an old photo of Mike. Could you bring your favorite photo of Mike from when he was in school?

Love,

Abby

Hi Abby,

Great to hear from you. Yes, we're well and we love our new house. We've just finished painting our bedroom, and we're going to start on the kitchen next weekend.

Thanks for inviting us to Mike's birthday party. We're free on the 21st and we'd love to come. I'll bring some really funny photos of Mike when he was in school! We're looking forward to seeing you and Mike.

All the best,

Tony

b Read the emails again. Are the sentences true or false?

1 Abby and Mike have seen Tony and Laura recently.
2 Tony and Laura have recently moved to a new house.
3 Abby wants Mike's friends to take photos of him at the restaurant.
4 Tony and Laura are making some changes to their new house.
5 Tony doesn't have any old photos of Mike.

2 WRITING SKILLS Inviting and replying

a Correct the sentences. Use contractions where possible.

1 Hope your well and enjoying your new job.
Hope you're well and enjoying your new job.
2 Thanks for invite me to your party.
______
3 It would be great to seeing you.
______
4 We're free on Saturday and we love to come.
______
5 We having a party on Saturday.
______
6 We didn't see you in ages!
______

3 WRITING

a Read Sam's email to Jess inviting her to his birthday party, and the notes below. Decide whether Jess can or can't go to the party and write her reply.

Hi Jess,

How are you? I haven't seen you for over six months. I hope you are well and enjoying your new job.

Are you doing anything next Saturday? I'm having a birthday party at my house, and I'm inviting a few friends. People are arriving at 7:30. Everyone is bringing some food for the party. Could you bring a salad?

It would be wonderful to see you and have a chance to talk.

Love,

Sam

Notes for reply:
She CAN go to the party

1 Me? Fine. Give information about new job
2 Thanks for invitation
3 Free next Sat, love to come
4 Bring a huge salad!
5 Looking forward

Notes for reply:
She CAN'T go to the party

1 Me? Fine. Give information about new job
2 Thanks for invitation
3 Party = fun! Can't come
4 Visit cousin in Vancouver next weekend
5 Enjoy the party!

Reading and listening extension

1 READING

a Read the magazine article. Put the events in the order that Julia does them.

- [ ] Arriving at the theater
- [ ] Getting a new outfit
- [ ] Going to the hairdresser's
- [ ] Having lunch
- [ ] Meeting my friend
- [1] Running on Venice Beach

b Read the magazine article again. Are the sentences true or false?

1 There are a lot of people on Venice Beach in the morning.
2 Julia thinks she will spend all day shopping.
3 There are a lot of people at the shopping mall.
4 Julia doesn't want to have lunch until she's bought a new dress.
5 Julia is looking forward to the evening because she has never been to a premiere before.

c Complete the sentences with the correct forms of the verbs in parentheses.

1 Julia _is meeting_ her friend at the shopping mall today. (meet)
2 At 1:15 Julia is ________ lunch. She ________ anything yet. (have, buy)
3 At 4:22 Julia ________ the hairdresser's in a taxi. (go)
4 At 6:35 Julia ________ to go out. (get ready)
5 At 7:15 she ________ at the theater. (arrive)

d Write an email to a friend about your plans for the weekend. Remember to include:

- where you are going
- what you are going to do
- who you are going with
- what you think will happen.

12 HOURS IN LOS ANGELES

with movie director Julia Fitzgerald

7:15 a.m. The sun is shining, and I'm going to put my tracksuit on and go for a run. I love this time of the day because it's so peaceful and quiet down on Venice Beach.

10:00 a.m. I'm going to a movie premiere tonight, so I have to look my best. I've planned to meet my friend at an indoor shopping mall in Santa Monica, but she's not here yet. It's a modern place with a lot of great stores and some pretty little cafés. I'd like to buy a new dress. It's crowded today, so I'm sure we'll be here all day!

1:15 p.m. We've stopped for lunch at an ordinary LA diner. I haven't bought anything yet, but all this walking around is making me hungry. I'm going to get a burger and fries.

2:20 p.m. My friend's taking me to a huge new department store that sells everything. She thinks we'll find something there.

3:05 p.m. Success! I found a gorgeous red dress and matching high heels. We've decided to celebrate with coffee and cake at my favorite outdoor café near the beach.

4:22 p.m. I'm in a taxi now. I have an appointment at the hairdresser's at 4:30 p.m. I hope I'm not late, but I think I might be!

6:35 p.m. I'm almost ready. Should I wear the gold bracelet and necklace or the black one? I can't decide. The car is coming at 7:00 p.m., so I have some time.

7:15 p.m. We're driving up to the theater for the premiere. It's crowded and noisy because everyone is hoping to see all the stars. It's my first time at a premiere, so I'm really excited. It's going to be a wonderful night!

2 LISTENING

a 04.07 Listen to the conversation. Complete the sentences with the names in the box.

Alex Marlon's mom Gavino ~~Marlon~~ Isaac

1 __Marlon__ is going to finish college this summer.
2 ______ is marrying an Italian woman.
3 ______ is teaching Marlon Italian next week.
4 ______ wants to go sightseeing in Rome.
5 ______ is going on a date tonight.

b 04.07 Listen to the conversation again and check (✓) the correct answers.

1 Why is Marlon going to Italy this summer?
  a ☑ He is going to a wedding.
  b ☐ His girlfriend is Italian.
  c ☐ He wants to visit Rome.
2 Who is Laura?
  a ☐ Marlon's girlfriend
  b ☐ Alex's fiancée
  c ☐ a student in their class
3 What is Marlon's dad going to do if Marlon does well in school?
  a ☐ He's going to pay for Italian lessons.
  b ☐ He's going to buy him a new suit.
  c ☐ He's going to take him to Rome.
4 What does Isaac like about Rome?
  a ☐ the new buildings
  b ☐ the history
  c ☐ the mix of old and new architecture
5 Where is Isaac going now?
  a ☐ He is going to work.
  b ☐ He is going to get a haircut.
  c ☐ He is going home.

c Write about what you're going to do when you finish your English class. Include the answers to these questions:

- Where are you going to go?
- What would you like to do?

Review and extension

1 GRAMMAR

Correct the sentences.

1 I going to look for a job in a hotel this summer.
I'm going to look for a job in a hotel this summer.
2 Don't worry. I pay the money back tomorrow.
3 He'll go to buy a new car next month.
4 Will I come to your house in half an hour?
5 Will we go to that café for some coffee?
6 Are you going to doing your homework tonight?

2 VOCABULARY

Correct the sentences.

1 There is a fantastic outside swimming pool in my town.
There is a fantastic outdoor swimming pool in my town.
2 Are you going to buy a new suit case on sale?
3 I love it here in the country. It's so peacefull!
4 He always uses a tie when he goes on a job interview.
5 I love coming to this park because you can't hear the traffic. It's so quite here.
6 That restaurant's so noise. It's really hard to talk there.

3 WORDPOWER *look*

Complete the sentences with the words in the box.

good forward up around ~~at~~ for

1 He looked __at__ the schedule to see when the next train left for London.
2 Excuse me. I'm looking ______ a bank. Is there one near here?
3 We're really looking ______ to seeing our Ecuadorian friends tomorrow.
4 Are you OK? You don't look ______.
5 I'm tired! Do you really want to look ______ the museum again?
6 If you're not sure what it means, look ______ the word in your dictionary.

REVIEW YOUR PROGRESS

Look again at Review Your Progress on p. 46 of the Student's Book. How well can you do these things now?
3 = very well 2 = well 1 = not so well

I CAN ...	
talk about plans for celebrations	☐
plan a day out in a city	☐
make social plans	☐
write and reply to an invitation.	☐

5A I HAVE TO WORK LONG HOURS

1 VOCABULARY Work

a Complete the sentences.

1 This person takes care of the plants and cuts the grass. gardener
2 When your hair gets too long, you make an appointment with this person. h__________
3 If you have a problem with your kitchen sink, you need to call this person. p__________
4 This person works in a laboratory and might have a college degree in chemistry or biology. s__________
5 Somebody whose job is to look after people's money. b__________
6 If you have a problem with the lights in your house, you call this person. e__________
7 If the police arrest you, this person can help you. l__________
8 This person can help you manage your money. a__________
9 This person cooks food in a restaurant. c__________
10 When you are in the hospital, this person takes care of you. n__________

b Complete the sentences with the words in the box.

team people environment self-employed skills salary college degree qualifications training ~~long hours~~

1 He's usually in his office from 8 a.m. until 8 p.m., but he doesn't mind working long hours.
2 She works for a large bank in Baltimore, earns a very good __________, and drives a company car.
3 You need to have several years of __________ after you study to become a doctor.
4 They have a really nice working __________ – their offices are modern with good air conditioning and plenty of light.
5 I really enjoy working on big projects with a lot of other people. It's good to work on a __________.
6 You need to have a __________ to become a lawyer.
7 Receptionists have to deal with __________, so they need to be friendly and polite.
8 Some people prefer to be __________ and work for a lot of different companies.
9 Secretaries need to have a lot of __________ – they need to be organized and good with computers.
10 You need to have good __________ if you want to get a job at this university.

2 GRAMMAR *must / have to / can*

a Complete the sentences about the signs with *have to* or *can't*.

1 You have to wash your hands before you go into this room.

2 Excuse me, ma'am. You __________ stand up until the plane has stopped.

3 I'm sorry, sir. You __________ take photos in here with a flash.

4 Excuse me. I'm afraid you __________ wear your seat belt all the time.

5 Visitors __________ wear hard hats when they come to this building site.

6 I'm sorry. You __________ smoke in the bathroom.

b Underline the correct words to complete the text.

I work as a receptionist in a big hotel, so I [1]*must / must not / can* always be polite to the guests. During the week, I [2]*don't have to / can't / must* go to bed late because I have to start work early. Fortunately, I [3]*don't have to / must not / can't* wear a uniform, but I [4]*can / must not / have to* dress professionally.

My sister's a student, so she [5]*must not / doesn't have to / can't* get up early most days. However, she [6]*doesn't have to / must not / has to* study very hard right now because she has important exams next month.

My dad's a taxi driver, so he often [7]*has to / must not / can't* work at night and on weekends. He [8]*doesn't have to / must not / must* drive fast because there are speed cameras everywhere on the city streets.

My mom's a nurse, so she [9]*has to / must not / can't* wear a uniform when she's at work. Sometimes she starts work very early, but my dad usually takes her to work in his taxi, so she [10]*must / doesn't have to / must not* take the bus.

5B I MIGHT GET A JOB TODAY!

1 GRAMMAR *will* and *might* for predictions

a Match 1–8 with a–h to make sentences.

1 [c] She might
2 [ ] I think I'll
3 [ ] Argentina might not
4 [ ] I don't think she'll
5 [ ] I'm sure he'll
6 [ ] Italy won't
7 [ ] He might not
8 [ ] I might not

a win the game on Saturday. The Brazilian team is just as good as them.
b pass his exams. He's very smart, and he's worked really hard all year.
c feel better tomorrow. She says she's taken some medicine.
d get to school on time. I just woke up!
e pass his exams. He hasn't worked very hard this year.
f win the game on Saturday. They don't have any good players on their team, and Argentina is a fantastic team.
g come this evening. She's not feeling well.
h see them tonight. We all usually go to the gym on Thursdays.

b Complete the sentences with *will* (or *'ll*), *won't*, *might*, or *might not*.

1 I'm sure you __will__ pass your exams. You've worked very hard this year.
2 Don't go on vacation next week. They ____________ ask you back for a second interview.
3 I know they ____________ offer me a good salary. A friend of mine works there, and he doesn't earn a lot of money.
4 You ____________ get a job immediately when you finish college – 50% of college graduates don't have a job three years after finishing their studies.
5 She doesn't think she ____________ travel after college. She wants to find a job as soon as possible.
6 **A** Do you think he ____________ pass all his exams?
B Yes, I'm sure he ____________. Don't worry.
7 Who knows? You ____________ make some useful contacts at the conference.
8 I'm sure he ____________ get the job. He doesn't have any experience.

2 VOCABULARY Jobs

a Write the names of the jobs under the pictures.

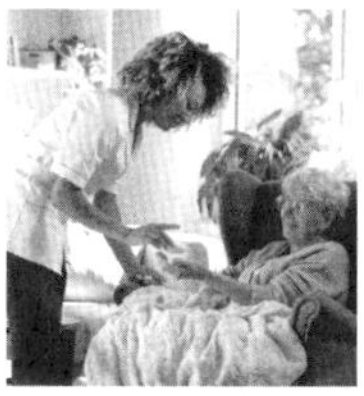
1 __caregiver__

2 ____________

3 ____________

4 ____________

5 ____________

6 ____________

7 ____________

8 ____________

9 ____________

10 ____________

11 ____________

12 ____________

b Complete the sentences with the correct jobs.

1 When I was little, I wanted to be a v__et__ because I loved taking care of animals.
2 I'm looking for a good c____________ to fix the roof on my house.
3 Nick is a fantastic m____________. He can play the piano, the guitar, the cello, and the saxophone.
4 Christopher Wren was the a____________ who designed St. Paul's Cathedral in London.
5 Michelle works in a department store as a s____________ a____________.
6 Chris Evans is an American movie a____________, famous for his role as Captain America in the Marvel Comics movies.
7 Adrian works as a c____________, taking care of old people in their homes.
8 Sarah works in our IT Department as a c____________ p____________.
9 James was a well-known j____________ who worked for *The New York Times*.
10 Yves St. Laurent was a famous French fashion d____________.
11 The t____________ d____________ works around downtown Miami from 8 p.m. to 5 a.m.
12 I hope that the p____________s in the UN can solve the world's problems one day.

5C EVERYDAY ENGLISH
I'll finish things here, if you want

1 USEFUL LANGUAGE
Offers and suggestions

a Put the words in the correct order to make sentences.

1 money / I / you / some / lend / the bus / for / should ?
Should I lend you some money for the bus?

2 off / maybe you / ask / manager / for / your / should / the day .
____

3 look up / the / I'll / train times / online .
____

4 do / a taxi / guest / you / our / me / to / want / for / call ?
____

5 drive / airport / don't / the / why / I / to / you ?
____

6 arranging / about / a / in / meeting / Mexico City / how ?
____

7 money / don't / why / borrow / from / some / you / your dad ?
____

8 Quebec / could / direct flight / you / a / to / catch .
____

b 05.01 Listen and check.

c Complete the sentences with the words in the box.

fine about could mind ~~should~~ sorry matter don't maybe would idea worry

1 **A** *Should* I book a room for your meeting?
B Yes, good ________.

2 **A** ________ you like me to drive you to the bus station?
B No, I'll be ________. Don't ________ about it. I can walk.

3 **A** But you won't be able to have any lunch.
B Oh, never ________. I'm not really hungry.

4 **A** I'm really ________. I can't go to the movies tonight.
B Oh, it doesn't ________. We can go another time.

5 How ________ asking your boss if you can have more time for the report?

6 Why ________ I book the train tickets online?

7 ________ you should invite your boss to the meeting, too?

8 You ________ send her some flowers for her birthday.

d 05.02 Listen and check.

2 PRONUNCIATION Stressed/unstressed modals: vowel sounds

a 05.03 Listen to the sentences. Is the modal verb in **bold** stressed or unstressed? Check (✓) the correct box.

	Stressed	Unstressed
1 **Would** you like some coffee?		✓
2 Yes, I **would**. Thanks.		
3 **Could** you help me with my report?		
4 Yes, of course I **could**.		
5 You **should** get a taxi.		
6 Yes, you're right. I **should**.		
7 **Should** you book a meeting room?		
8 Well, what do you think? **Should** I?		

5D SKILLS FOR WRITING
I am writing to apply for a job

1 READING

a Read the job ad and Martin's job application, and check (✓) the correct answer.

a ☐ The job is for 12 months.
b ☐ The job is in a hotel in Denver.
c ☐ The hotel needs a receptionist.
d ☐ The hotel needs a server.

b Read the job ad and job application again. Are the sentences true or false?

1 The hotel will give the receptionist a bedroom and food.
2 People who apply for this job don't need experience working in hotels.
3 Martin is free to work this winter.
4 Martin would like to learn some new skills.
5 Martin doesn't have any previous experience working in hotels.
6 Martin would like more details about the job.

2 WRITING SKILLS Organizing an email

a Match 1–8 with a–h to make sentences.

1 [g] I'm writing to
2 ☐ I have five years'
3 ☐ I would like to work for your company
4 ☐ I have a lot of experience
5 ☐ My experience working in a busy hospital
6 ☐ My résumé is attached with
7 ☐ Could you please send me information
8 ☐ I look forward to

a working on a team and dealing with customers.
b about the working hours and training program?
c more information about my past employment.
d because it would be a good opportunity to learn some new skills.
e hearing from you.
f experience working as a secretary in a busy hospital.
g apply for the job of secretary.
h will be very useful for this job.

DENVER CHRONICLE – classifieds

HOTEL RECEPTIONIST WANTED

We're looking for a hardworking and friendly receptionist to work in a hotel in Aspen this winter. You will need to speak a foreign language.

We prefer someone with experience working in hotels.

Accommodation and meals provided.

Apply online at www.aspenlodge.com by November 15.

Subject: Hotel Receptionist

Dear Sir/Madam,

I am writing to apply for the job of receptionist at the Aspen Lodge, which you advertised in the *Denver Chronicle*.

I am studying French and Spanish online through the University of Colorado and am available to work in the winter.

I would like to work for you because it would be a good opportunity for me to learn new skills and to work on a team. I have worked in a hotel before as a server, so I have experience dealing with customers and working in a busy hotel environment.

My résumé is attached with details of my previous experience.

Could you please send me information about the salary, the working hours, and the accommodation?

I look forward to hearing from you.

Sincerely,

Martin Evans

3 WRITING

a Read the job ad and write a letter applying for the job.

The Daily – classifieds

SALES ASSISTANT WANTED

T-World is looking for a hardworking sales assistant to sell all types of computers, tablets, game consoles, smart TVs, and smartphones in our brand-new superstore in Charleston.

We are offering a good salary plus sales bonus to the right person.

You will need previous sales experience and a good understanding of the latest technology.

We prefer someone with experience working in a busy environment.

Full training program given.

Apply by September 30 salesassistant@tworld.com

UNIT 5

Reading and listening extension

1 READING

a Read the article. Match the people 1–4 with pictures a–d.

1 ☐ Malcolm
2 ☐ Freya
3 ☐ Cara
4 ☐ James

a 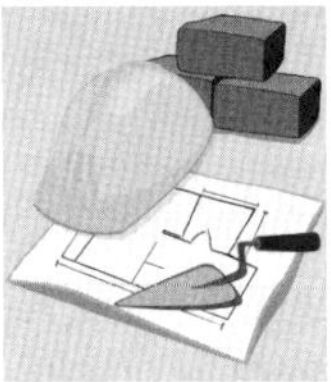 b  c 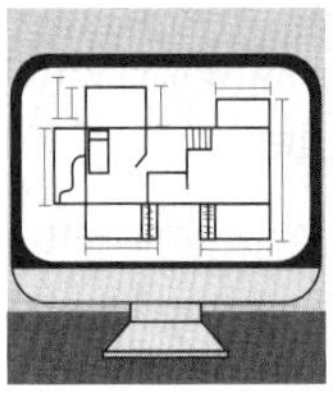 d 

b Read the article again and check (✓) the correct boxes. Sometimes there is more than one possible answer.

	Gets paid well	Works and studies	Is doing something they love	Has to work many hours every day
1 Malcolm		✓		
2 Freya				
3 Cara				
4 James				

c Read the article again and underline the correct answer. Sometimes there is more than one possible answer.

1 Who works for themselves?
a Malcolm b Freya c Cara d James
2 Who doesn't earn any money?
a Malcolm b Freya c Cara d James
3 Who has the weekends free?
a Malcolm b Freya c Cara d James
4 Who likes the place where they work?
a Malcolm b Freya c Cara d James
5 Who studies and works in a different place?
a Malcolm b Freya c Cara d James

d Write a paragraph about a job you'd like to do. Remember to include:

- the things you'd like to do at the job
- the hours
- the salary
- the environment.

Where to now?

When you finish school or college, you must think carefully about what you would like to do next. Here, some young people tell us their experiences.

I thought about my skills and qualifications, and then about me. I've always liked working on a team, I like being outside, and I decided I can't work in an office every day. Someone suggested I train to be a construction worker. I go to classes Monday and Friday, and I work Tuesday to Thursday. I have to get up early, so I can't go out at night, but I'm learning a useful skill.

Malcolm, 19

I work for a number of companies as a book designer. I'm self-employed, which means I work on my own and not on a team. When I'm very busy, I have to work long hours, in the evenings, and sometimes on weekends. But I really like my job, and I can work at home, so I can say that I have a really nice working environment! I don't have to deal with customers or a manager! When I'm busy, I can earn really good money, but I'm not always busy.

Cara, 28

I love art and design, and I've always wanted to do something I enjoy. I decided to study to become an architect. I'm learning so much, and I'm doing what I want, which is really important. I have to study every day of the week, and I just hope I can find a job when I finish college.

Freya, 21

I've always liked animals. Earning a really good salary is important to me too, so I studied to be a vet. I have to work long hours, and I have to study at home most weekends, but I know it is worth it when I'm helping sick animals.

James, 24

2 LISTENING

a 05.04 Listen to the conversation. What did Josh say about these jobs? Check (✓) the correct boxes. Sometimes there is more than one possible answer.

	Construction worker	Hairdresser	IT worker	Bank teller
1 Work long hours	✓			
2 Nice working environment				
3 Deal with people				
4 Earn a good salary				
5 Work on a team				

b 05.04 Listen to the conversation again, and complete the chart to show what Josh liked and disliked about the jobs. Write one word in each space.

	He liked ...	He disliked ...
1 Construction worker	working *outside*.	starting work ______.
2 Hairdresser	learning new ______.	dealing with ______.
3 IT worker	______ work when he wanted.	working on ______.

c Choose one of the following:

1 Write a conversation between two people. Person A is interviewing Person B for the job of a journalist. Person B explains why he/she is the right person for the job, and asks five questions about the job. Person A asks questions and answers the questions Person B asks.
2 Write about the parts of a job you would be happy to do, and what you definitely wouldn't like to do.

Review and extension

1 GRAMMAR

Correct the sentences.

1 Tomorrow's Sunday, so I must not get up early.
Tomorrow's Sunday, so I don't have to get up early.
2 Excuse me, sir. You don't have to eat in the laboratory. It's against the rules.
3 Do you must wear a suit to work?
4 When I finish school, I can go to college. It depends on my grades.
5 I've to start work at 7 o'clock in the morning at my new job!
6 I'll take my umbrella. It can rain this afternoon.

2 VOCABULARY

Correct the sentences.

1 At your new job, I'm sure they'll give you a lot of trainings.
At your new job, I'm sure they'll give you a lot of training.
2 My sister works as a sales assistent in a big department store.
3 You need good qualification if you want to become a doctor.
4 He works as a disigner for a top fashion magazine.
5 If you want to become a plummer, you'll need to do a training program.
6 My brother wants to become a professional music.

3 WORDPOWER *job* and *work*

Underline the correct words to complete the sentences.

1 The GPS on my phone doesn't *work* / *job* very well when I drive through the mountains.
2 I've found a really good *job* / *work* at the local newspaper.
3 No, I can't go to the movies. I have to stay late at *job* / *work*.
4 My headache's a little better, so I think that medicine's beginning to *work* / *job*.
5 What time do you start *job* / *work* in the morning?
6 He has to *work* / *job* all weekend on that report.
7 I'm studying for my final exams – it's really hard *job* / *work*.
8 My dad has a lot of small *jobs* / *works* to do in the yard.
9 My dad can't *work* / *job* out because he hurt his back last week.

REVIEW YOUR PROGRESS

Look again at Review Your Progress on p. 56 of the Student's Book. How well can you do these things now?
3 = very well 2 = well 1 = not so well

I CAN ...	
talk about what people do at work	☐
talk about my future career	☐
make offers and suggestions	☐
write a job application.	☐

6A YOU SHOULD TAKE A BREAK

1 GRAMMAR Imperative; *should*

a Complete the text with the words in the box.

should go   don't use   eat   should read   shouldn't drink
go   don't sit   should have   shouldn't have   ~~get~~

Here are some ideas for those of you who have problems sleeping:

First of all, 1 _get_ plenty of exercise during the day. For example, 2 ________ for a long walk at lunchtime or after work. 3 ________ at home watching TV all night. Second, you 4 ________ dinner late in the evening. 5 ________ dinner at least four hours before you go to bed. Also, you 6 ________ coffee after 4 p.m. – it will stop you from sleeping. Next, 7 ________ your laptop when you're in bed. Instead, you 8 ________ a good book at bedtime – it's very relaxing. Also, some people find it hard to sleep if their room isn't dark enough, so you 9 ________ thick curtains in your bedroom so that the light doesn't wake you up too early in the morning. Finally, you 10 ________ to bed at the same time every night. Doing this tells your body that it's time for you to go to sleep. Sweet dreams, everyone!

b Correct the sentences. Use *should*, *shouldn't*, or the imperative.

1 He shouldn't listening to music while he's studying.
He shouldn't listen to music while he's studying.
2 To eat a lot of fruit and vegetables every day.
____
3 Not use your computer for very long at night.
____
4 You should to try to relax for an hour before you go to bed.
____
5 I think she should getting more exercise during the day.
____
6 You don't should go swimming immediately after lunch.
____
7 When you have a headache, to drink water.
____
8 Don't stay you at work after six o'clock.
____

2 VOCABULARY Verbs with dependent prepositions

a Match 1–8 with a–h to make sentences.

1 [e] When you called me, I was looking
2 [ ] The train from Philadelphia arrived
3 [ ] Can you think
4 [ ] He was listening
5 [ ] Could you deal
6 [ ] He asked his father
7 [ ] Matthew decided to talk
8 [ ] My father wants to pay

a for $50 because he needed a new shirt for the wedding.
b to his son's teacher about his grades.
c for lunch with his credit card.
d of a nice present for your grandpa's birthday?
e at an old photo of when we were in school.
f with this order for six pizzas to go, please?
g to the baseball game on the radio.
h at Union Station 25 minutes late.

b Underline the correct words to complete the sentences.

1 In my job, I have to deal *about* / *for* / *with* customers all day long.
2 It's hard to concentrate *with* / *on* / *for* my homework when you're listening to the radio.
3 This bus is crowded! I'll wait *for* / *to* / *from* the next one.
4 His girlfriend's gone to Paris for a month, so he thinks *from* / *about* / *for* her all the time.
5 They don't pay you a lot do they? You should ask your boss *from* / *on* / *for* a raise.
6 Jackie says she spends about $200 a month *at* / *on* / *to* clothes!
7 If you want to buy a new car now, you should borrow some money *with* / *for* / *from* the bank.
8 He's really generous. He paid *with* / *for* / *of* my plane ticket to New York!

3 PRONUNCIATION Sound and spelling: /u/ and /ʊ/

a 06.01 Listen to the sentences. Are the vowel sounds in **bold** /u/ or /ʊ/? Check (✓) the correct box for each sentence.

	/u/	/ʊ/
1 We t**oo**k my grandma to the theater.	☐	✓
2 The children wanted to go to the z**oo**.	☐	☐
3 Where did you l**o**se your cell phone?	☐	☐
4 W**ou**ld you like some coffee?	☐	☐
5 Wh**o** did you invite to the party?	☐	☐
6 I don't think you sh**ou**ld go to work today.	☐	☐
7 C**ou**ld I borrow $5, please?	☐	☐
8 What did you think of the f**oo**d?	☐	☐

6B I WAS VERY FRIGHTENED

1 VOCABULARY *-ed / -ing* adjectives

a Underline the correct words to complete the sentences.

1 I thought the New York City subway was really *confused / confusing*. There are too many subway lines!
2 The soccer game was very *exciting / excited*. It finished 4 – 4.
3 Tracy isn't very *interesting / interested* in video games.
4 I was *shocked / shocking* when I saw him. He looked really sick.
5 She was very *annoyed / annoying* when he asked her for some more money.
6 The flight from London to Mexico City was very *tired / tiring*.
7 I thought the view from the top of the Eiffel Tower was *amazing / amazed*.
8 He felt *embarrassing / embarrassed* when his mom kissed him in front of his friends.

b Complete the sentences with adjectives ending in *-ed* or *-ing*.

1 The people in the apartment above me are so a<u>nnoying</u>. They play loud music when I'm trying to go to sleep.
2 He looked really c__________ when he woke up. He said, "Where am I?"
3 I thought that documentary about Martin Luther King Jr. was really i__________.
4 The exam results were very s__________. Nobody got higher than 50%!
5 She was very f__________ when she saw the spider, but she calmed down when we told her it was plastic.
6 He was very d__________ that his father didn't bring him a present from Spain.
7 They couldn't speak a word when they heard the s__________ news that the singer was dead.
8 She felt very e__________ when he told her that they were going on vacation to Florida.

2 GRAMMAR Uses of the infinitive

a Put the words in the correct order to make sentences.

1 job / I / to / disappointed / get / not / was / the .
<u>I was disappointed not to get the job.</u>
2 sharks / was / learn / interesting / it / to / about .
____
3 our cars / you / tell us / park / where / can / to ?
____
4 wear / is / not / dangerous / to / a seat belt / it .
____
5 her / relax / to / she / a bath / help / took .
____
6 the bus station / went / to / meet / aunt / to / they / their .
____
7 her father / she / him / to / some money / ask / for / called .
____
8 didn't / he / what / to the party / know / wear / to .
____

b Correct the sentences.

1 They wanted buy him a nice birthday present.
<u>They wanted to buy him a nice birthday present.</u>
2 He asked me how getting to the airport.
____
3 She was annoyed to not receive an invitation to his wedding.
____
4 They went to the supermarket for buy some food for dinner.
____
5 We couldn't remember which bus catching to the airport.
____
6 John and Angela decided to have not their wedding in Hawaii.
____
7 It was embarrassing fail my driving test again.
____
8 She went to the library for borrow a book on dinosaurs for her son.
____

6C EVERYDAY ENGLISH
What do you think I should do?

1 USEFUL LANGUAGE
Asking for and giving advice

a Match sentences 1–8 with responses a–h.

1 [d] I think it's a good idea to reserve a table. The restaurant might be full.
2 [ ] Someone stole my bag when I was at the beach this afternoon.
3 [ ] I'd talk to your boss about it.
4 [ ] I wouldn't worry too much. You can get a new passport at the embassy.
5 [ ] Do you think I should invite Jorge to the surprise party?
6 [ ] What do you think I should do?
7 [ ] I didn't get the job in marketing.
8 [ ] I broke my finger on Saturday.

a Oh, that's too bad. I'm sure you'll get another job soon.
b Oh, that's a shame. So that means you can't play tennis today?
c No, I don't think that's a very good idea. Anna doesn't like him very much.
d Yes, I guess so. Saturday night can be very busy.
e How awful! I'm really sorry to hear that.
f I don't think I should do that. She'll be mad at me.
g Yes, you're right. I can go there one day next week.
h I think you should go to the police station.

b 06.02 Listen and check.

c Put the words in the correct order to make sentences.

1 apply for / which / should / do / job / you / I / think ?
Which job do you think I should apply for?
2 coworkers / should / I / your / you / think / ask .
____
3 sorry / really / that / hear / to / I'm .
____
4 new job / a / should / do / think / I / you / look / for ?
____
5 I / a / think it's / to / your boss / talk / to / good idea .
____
6 about / talk / I'd / your parents / it / to .
____
7 apply / I / for / marketing job / new / the / wouldn't .
____
8 think / I / you / your / don't / job / leave / should .
____

d 06.03 Listen and check.

2 PRONUNCIATION Main stress

a 06.04 Listen to the sentences and check (✓) the stressed words.

1 You're from Canada, right?
a [ ] You're b [✓] Canada
2 Elena works at the Spanish Embassy.
a [ ] Spanish b [ ] Embassy
3 Would you like to work in Houston?
a [ ] work b [ ] Houston
4 We're having a surprise party for Anna.
a [ ] party b [ ] Anna
5 My boss wants to talk to me.
a [ ] boss b [ ] me

6D SKILLS FOR WRITING
I often worry about tests and exams

1 READING

a Read Anthony's email to Marina and Marina's reply. Check (✓) the correct answer.

a ☐ Anthony is looking for a new job.
b ☐ Anthony doesn't want Jim to leave his job.
c ☐ Marina gives Anthony some ideas to help him.
d ☐ Marina works as a manager of a bank in Cleveland.

Dear Marina,

The problem is that I'm feeling very stressed about my job right now. You see, Jim, one of the people on my team, has just left. They haven't replaced Jim yet, so my boss has given all of his work to the other people on the team, including me. Do you have any advice for me?

Sincerely,

Anthony

Dear Anthony,

Thank you for your email. I'm very pleased that you have written to me for advice.

This kind of situation is very common in companies when somebody leaves. I remember this happened when I was working at a bank in Cleveland. One summer, two of the people on my team left the bank at the same time. We had to do all of their work, and it took three months to replace them! Anyway, here are some ideas that might help you.

First of all, try not to get too stressed about the situation. I think you should discuss the problem with your coworkers. Maybe they will have some ideas about how to make the situation a little easier? Second, when you have too much work to do, I think it's a good idea to try to prioritize your work carefully. For example, are there some less urgent jobs that you could do later?

Next, I think you should talk to your boss about this problem. He might not realize how much work he has given you, and maybe he can find some other people to help you with it. Finally, I'd try to do something relaxing after work, such as going to the gym or going swimming. It's important to relax when you're not at work and to get plenty of sleep.

I hope this helps you, and please feel free to come and talk to me in my office.

Best,

Marina Rodriguez

HR Manager

b Read the emails again. Are the sentences true or false?

1 Anthony is doing all of Jim's work.
2 Marina was the manager of a team of two people at the bank.
3 Marina thinks that Anthony should talk to his coworkers about the problem.
4 Marina doesn't think Anthony should discuss the problem with his manager.
5 Marina thinks it's a good idea for Anthony to relax after work.

2 WRITING SKILLS Linking: ordering ideas and giving examples

a Put *for example* or *such as* in the correct place in each sentence. Add capital letters and punctuation (. , ') and make any other necessary changes.

1 There are lots of ways to make new friends joining a sports club.
There are lots of ways to make new friends, such as joining a sports club.
2 It's a good idea to read something in English every day. You can read different newspapers online.
____
3 Why don't you do something relaxing this evening going for a swim after work?
____
4 There are more enjoyable ways to prepare for an exam. You could study with a friend who's in the same class.
____
5 You could start a new hobby to help you relax dancing or swimming.
____

3 WRITING

a Read Kento's message to his English teacher, Tina. Use the notes below to write Tina's reply.

Dear Tina,

I think I'm pretty good at reading and writing in English, but listening is very hard for me. I really want to improve my listening. Do you have any ideas?

Thank you,

Kento

Notes for message to Kento:
Paragraph 1: say thanks
Paragraph 2: me: learning Japanese – listening v. difficult – explain why – ideas to help ...
Paragraph 3:
1) impossible to understand every word – concentrate on most important words
2) extra practice – learning center – listening exercises, e.g., listening tracks from Student's Book
3) radio / TV in English, movies (+ subtitles)
4) podcasts – short stories?
5) pop songs + read words – find websites
Paragraph 4: hope this helps – talk to me after class?

Reading and listening extension

1 READING

a Read the magazine article and <u>underline</u> the correct people to match the adjectives.

1	annoyed	*Petra / <u>manager</u> / Eva*
2	embarrassed	*Petra / customers / Eva*
3	confused	*manager / Eva / Petra*
4	frightened	*Petra / manager / customers*
5	not disappointed	*customers / Petra / Eva*
6	surprised	*Petra / customers / Eva*

b Read the magazine article again. Check (✓) the correct answers.

1 What is Petra's problem?
   a [ ] She doesn't like spending time with customers.
   b [✓] Her manager thinks she works too slowly.
   c [ ] She gets confused by what the customers say to her.

2 Who is Toni?
   a [ ] one of Petra's customers
   b [ ] Petra's manager
   c [ ] another hairdresser

3 When does Petra get embarrassed?
   a [ ] when her manager gets angry with her in front of customers
   b [ ] when the customers talk to her
   c [ ] when her manager looks at her

4 What surprises Eva?
   a [ ] Toni talks to Petra in front of customers.
   b [ ] Toni doesn't understand the customers.
   c [ ] Toni doesn't understand what good customer service is.

5 What advice does Eva give?
   a [ ] She thinks Petra should tell her manager how she feels.
   b [ ] She tells Petra not to think about it.
   c [ ] She thinks that Petra's customers should talk to Toni.

c Read the magazine article again. Match 1–5 with a–e to make sentences.

1 [*c*] Petra thinks that a customer who
2 [ ] Toni thinks that Petra
3 [ ] Petra can't concentrate when Toni
4 [ ] Petra is confused because she
5 [ ] Eva thinks that Toni

a keeps looking at her.
b shouldn't spend so much time talking to customers.
c spends a lot of money should get good service.
d thinks she is very good at her job.
e will change his mind after the customers talk to him.

d Write an email to Petra giving her some advice about her problem. Remember to include:

- some advice
- some instructions
- a similar situation from your own life.

Ask — Eva —

Every week, our experts answer your problems. This week, Eva Perez, our writer and management expert, answers a question about a problem at work.

Dear Eva,

I need to ask you for some help.

I'm a hairdresser, and I work in a very fashionable salon. I'm very good at dealing with the customers, and I like to talk to them when I cut their hair. They pay a lot of money for their haircuts, and I think it's important to spend time with them and make sure they're happy. But my manager, a man named Toni, gets really annoyed with me and keeps telling me to work faster. He sometimes talks to me in front of the customers, which makes me really embarrassed. He looks at me all the time when I talk to them, and now I find it really difficult to concentrate on what I'm doing.

I'm really confused. I'm a really good hairdresser. None of the customers are ever disappointed with my work, and I get along well with all my coworkers. I'm frightened of losing my job if I say anything.

Can you help me?

Petra

Dear Petra,

You're right. When customers spend a lot of money on a haircut, they should enjoy the experience, feel relaxed, and get excellent service. I'm surprised Toni doesn't understand this. How many of your customers would come back if you spent less than 15 minutes with them?

I think you should ask your customers for help. Ask them to talk to or write an email to your manager telling him what they like about the service you give them. I think your manager will soon change his mind.

Good luck!

Eva

2 LISTENING

a 06.05 Listen to three friends talking about studying. Check (✓) the people that match the statements.

	Elena	Madison	Max
1 I can't study at home.	✓		
2 I study at the library.			
3 I don't have a good memory.			
4 I listen to a recording of myself to help me remember.			
5 I can help someone with their studying.			

b 06.05 Listen to the three friends talk about studying again. Check (✓) the correct answers.

1 What is Elena's problem?
- a ☑ Her brother is disturbing her.
- b ☐ She doesn't have a laptop to use for studying.
- c ☐ She doesn't want to go to the library to study.

2 What does Max suggest Elena do?
- a ☐ She should go to the library to study.
- b ☐ She needs to tell someone to stop.
- c ☐ She should ask her parents to help her with the problem.

3 What is Elena going to do?
- a ☐ Talk to someone about the problem.
- b ☐ Go somewhere else to avoid the problem.
- c ☐ Talk to someone and go somewhere else.

4 Who has a problem with history?
- a ☐ Elena
- b ☐ Max
- c ☐ Madison

5 What is Elena embarrassed about?
- a ☐ Her poor memory.
- b ☐ Making a song to help her study.
- c ☐ Her grade on the physics exam.

6 What is Madison's problem?
- a ☐ She is confused by a subject.
- b ☐ She doesn't want to study a subject.
- c ☐ She has to take a subject again next year.

c Write to somebody giving advice about how he or she can get better grades on an exam.

Review and extension

1 GRAMMAR

Correct the sentences.

1 You shouldn't to drink coffee before you go to bed.
You shouldn't drink coffee before you go to bed.
2 I think he should doing some exercise every day.
3 You should read a book for to help you relax.
4 She asked me drive her to the train station.
5 My father taught me how play the guitar.
6 What I should do if I can't sleep well?

2 VOCABULARY

Correct the sentences.

1 The soccer game was really excited. It finished 3 – 3.
The soccer game was really exciting. It finished 3 – 3.
2 I was thinking in that TV show I saw last night.
3 My uncle paid the tickets and bought popcorn for us as well.
4 I can't afford to spend a lot of money in a vacation this year.
5 My little sister isn't very interesting in fashion.
6 I didn't hear the phone because I was listening some music.
7 I didn't think that horror movie was frightened. What about you?
8 I didn't have any money, so I had to borrow $20 to my brother.

3 WORDPOWER verb + *to*

Complete the sentences with the words in the box.

read sold paid wrote lent
described ~~explained~~ brought

1 She *explained* the problem to her parents.
2 I ______ $200 to Jack so he could buy a phone.
3 He ______ a lot of food to the party.
4 Gianni ______ an email to the school asking for information about their language classes.
5 We ______ $500 to the construction worker who fixed our roof.
6 She ______ the story very quietly to her class, closed the book, and put it back on the shelf.
7 They ______ their car to their neighbor for $1,500.
8 Laura ______ her new house in Australia to me.

REVIEW YOUR PROGRESS

Look again at Review Your Progress on p. 66 of the Student's Book. How well can you do these things now?
3 = very well 2 = well 1 = not so well

I CAN ...	
give advice for common problems	☐
describe extreme experiences	☐
ask for and give advice	☐
write an email giving advice.	☐

7A I'M THE HAPPIEST I'VE EVER BEEN

1 GRAMMAR
Comparatives and superlatives

a Read the information in the chart about London, New York, and Buenos Aires. Complete the sentences with the correct forms of the adjectives in parentheses.

	London	New York	Buenos Aires
Average max. daily temperature: January	8°C	3°C	29°C
Average max. daily temperature: July	23°C	29°C	15°C
Population	8.9 million	8.6 million	2.8 million
Size	1,500 km²	1,200 km²	203 km²
Average hotel price	$167	$247	$64

1 In July, London's not as __warm__ as New York. (warm)
2 Buenos Aires is the ________ city in January. (hot)
3 New York is ________ than London in January. (cold)
4 Buenos Aires is less ________ than New York in January. (cold)
5 Buenos Aires has the ________ population. (small)
6 Buenos Aires isn't as ________ as London. (big)
7 London is ________ than New York. (large)
8 Hotels in New York are ________ than hotels in Buenos Aires. (expensive)

b Put the words in the correct order to make sentences.

1 job / as / isn't / new / my old one / interesting / my / as .
My new job isn't as interesting as my old one.
2 movie / it's / the / seen / exciting / ever / I've / most / I think .
____
3 happier / is / ever / she's / than / my sister / been .
____
4 to understand her / more / she speaks / quickly / because / you / it's hard / than .
____
5 one of / best / he / the U.S. / universities / to / in / went / the .
____
6 was / much warmer / the weather's / yesterday / it / than .
____
7 her sister / than / she / got / and / worked / on her exam / 95% / harder .
____
8 a year ago / English / speaks / than / much better / now / he .
____

2 VOCABULARY *get* collocations

a Underline the correct words to complete the sentences.

1 I *get together* / *get to know* / *get along well with* both of my sisters – we're very close.
2 I'm going to Australia on business next week, so I'll *get married* / *get in touch with* / *get to know* my friend Chris, who lives in Sydney.
3 In 2003, he married a Japanese woman and decided to stay in Japan because he *got a place at* / *got a job* / *got an offer* as a language teacher in Tokyo.
4 When she went to live in Burlington, she *got to know* / *got better* / *got engaged* her neighbors very quickly because everyone was so friendly.
5 Annie and Luis *got better* / *got divorced* / *got together* after they met at a friend's birthday two years ago. It was love at first sight.
6 If you don't drink bottled water, you might *get sick* / *get better* / *get old* because the water's not very clean here.
7 At my company, we normally *get rich* / *get paid* / *get an offer* on the last day of the month.
8 My parents *got married* / *got divorced* / *got engaged* last year, but they are still good friends.

b Complete the sentences with the correct forms of the expressions in the box.

get engaged   get rich   ~~get better~~   get paid
get to know   get accepted   get an offer   get married

1 Josh broke his leg playing soccer last year. Luckily, he __got better__ very quickly, and he's going skiing next month!
2 My parents ________ in 1995, and I was born in 1998.
3 He bought her a beautiful silver ring when they ________ last month.
4 You might ________ to Harvard University if you study very hard and do really well on your exams.
5 He ________ when he sold his software company to Google five years ago.
6 Emma was working as a model in Paris when she ________ to be in a French movie.
7 We ________ a lot of really interesting people when we lived in San Francisco.
8 Brad Pitt ________ over $20 million for his last movie.

7B I DIDN'T USE TO EAT HEALTHY FOOD

1 VOCABULARY Health collocations

a Match 1–8 with a–h to make sentences.

1 [c] She gave up
2 [ ] I've lost a lot of
3 [ ] I'm sure he's put on
4 [ ] My plan is to get
5 [ ] A lot of teenagers today are
6 [ ] She keeps in
7 [ ] It's important to have a healthy
8 [ ] I was a regular

a shape by exercising regularly and eating healthily.
b fit by going to the gym twice a week starting in January.
c junk food three years ago and now feels much healthier.
d overweight because they don't get enough exercise.
e smoker for ten years, but now I've stopped.
f weight since I started eating a healthy diet.
g weight because he doesn't look as thin as he did last year.
h diet with plenty of vegetables and fruit.

b Complete the sentences with the words in the box.

lose get gave up ~~keeps~~ gone put on allergies smoker overweight healthy

1 She keeps in shape by going to the gym twice a week and running.
2 He ________ a lot of weight a year ago. Now he's on a ________ diet, and he looks fitter.
3 Have you ever ________ on a diet to ________ weight?
4 If you go swimming three times a week, you'll ________ fit very quickly.
5 My uncle sleeps better because he ________ drinking coffee last month.
6 His doctor told him he was ________ and that he should lose ten kilos.
7 Do you have any ________ to certain types of food, such as seafood or peanuts?
8 She was a regular ________ for a long time, but she suddenly decided to stop last year.

2 GRAMMAR *used to*

a Rewrite the highlighted phrases. Use the correct forms of *used to*.

Twenty years ago, when I was a student, I use to live [1] I used to live in a large house with five of my friends. We usedn't to have [2] ________ much money, so we didn't used to go [3] ________ out to restaurants or clubs at night.

Instead, we use to invite [4] ________ our friends to come to our house in the evenings. One of my friends, Sandro, was Italian, and he use to cook [5] ________ fantastic meals for us, such as pizza or pasta. After dinner, we used watch [6] ________ TV or listen to music together.

Another friend of mine, Jordi, used play [7] ________ the guitar and teach us beautiful Spanish folk songs. Fortunately, our neighbors not used to complain [8] ________ about the noise we made.

What about you? Used you to live [9] ________ with a group of friends when you were in college, or you used to live [10] ________ with your family?

b Complete the sentences with the correct forms of *used to* and the verbs in parentheses.

1 We used to have a dog, but it died five years ago. (have)
2 Molly ________ bread from the supermarket, but now she has to get it there because her favorite bakery closed last month. (buy)
3 What ________ you ________ for lunch when you were in school? (eat)
4 She ________ German pretty well, but she hasn't spoken it for ten years, so she's forgotten most of it. (speak)
5 I ________ the bus to work every day, but now I usually ride my bike or walk. (take)
6 ________ you ________ with dolls when you were little? (play)
7 My grandfather ________ a cell phone, but he has one now. (have)
8 We ________ black-and-white movies at the movie theater when I was young. We thought they were great! (watch)

7C EVERYDAY ENGLISH
It hurts all the time

1 USEFUL LANGUAGE
Describing symptoms; Doctors' questions

a Match the doctor's sentences 1–8 with the patient's responses a–h.

1 [d] So, what's the problem?
2 [ ] When did this start?
3 [ ] Where does it hurt? Can you show me?
4 [ ] Can I take a look? So, does it hurt here?
5 [ ] Are you taking anything for the pain?
6 [ ] Well, I don't think it's anything to worry about.
7 [ ] I think it's just indigestion.
8 [ ] I'll give you a prescription for some medicine. Take two pills every four hours.

a Just indigestion? What a relief!
b OK. Thank you, Doctor.
c Phew! That's good to hear.
d I have a stomachache. It's really painful.
e Yes, it does. It hurts all the time. I can't get to sleep.
f Yes, I've taken some ibuprofen.
g About two days ago.
h Here, in this area.

b 07.01 Listen and check.

c Complete the sentences with the words in the box.

relief taking ~~worry~~ you problem hear ~~nothing~~ sick hurts look shouldn't get

1 Don't _worry_. It's _nothing_ to worry about.
2 Phew! That's good to ________.
3 It ________ all the time. I can't ________ to sleep.
4 Can I take a ________?
5 Are you ________ anything for the pain?
6 I feel ________ and exhausted.
7 I think ________ need to see another doctor.
8 So, what's the ________?
9 What a ________!
10 You ________ stay in bed.

d 07.02 Listen and check.

e Put the conversation in the correct order.

[ ] Yes! Very much. Is it broken?
[ ] OK, Doctor. Thank you.
[ ] Can you show me where it hurts?
[1] So, what brings you here today?
[ ] Does it hurt if I touch it here?
[ ] Right here, next to my wrist.
[ ] I hurt my arm. I fell off my bike.
[ ] No, I don't think so. I'll put a bandage on it.

2 PRONUNCIATION
Tones for asking questions

a 07.03 Listen to the questions. Check (✓) to show if the doctor's voice goes up ↗ or down ↘ at the end.

		↗	↘
1	Do you exercise?	✓	
2	When did this problem start?		
3	Could you have a few tests tomorrow?		
4	How much ibuprofen have you taken?		
5	How long have you had this problem?		
6	Are you taking anything for the pain?		
7	Do you have any allergies?		
8	Have you had any accidents recently?		

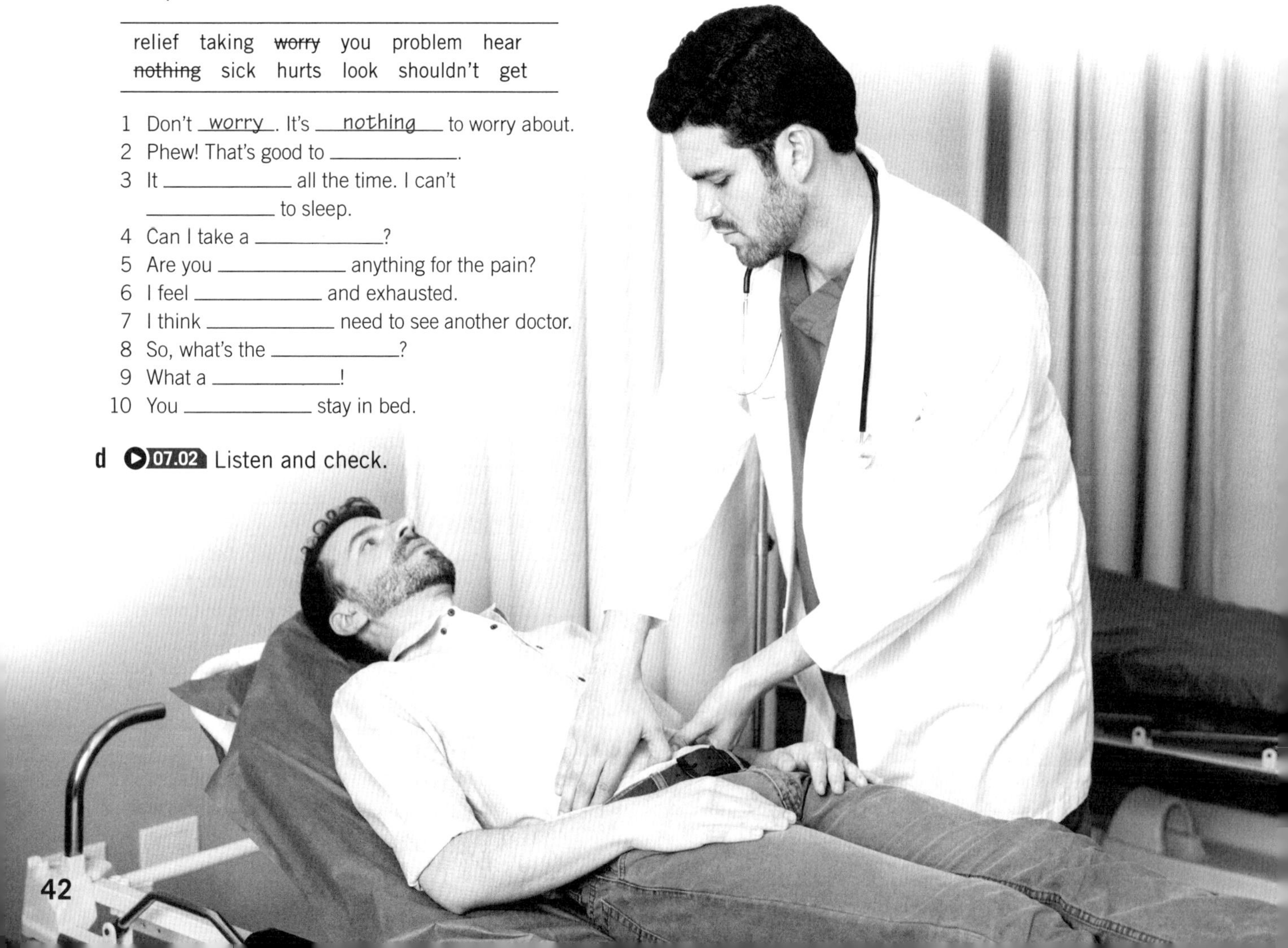

7D SKILLS FOR WRITING
After that, I decided to make a change

1 READING

a Read Nicola's blog on the right and check (✓) the correct answer.

a ☐ Nicola could speak Spanish very well two years ago.
b ☐ Nicola lives and works in Santiago.
c ☐ Nicola wanted to get a new job as a manager.
d ☐ Nicola studied Spanish in college.

b Read the blog again. Are the sentences true or false?

1 Two years ago, Nicola didn't get along well with her coworkers at the bank.
2 Managers at Nicola's bank need to have a very good level of Spanish.
3 Nicola used to buy a Spanish newspaper every day.
4 Nicola studied Spanish at a language school in Santiago.
5 Nicola is going to work for her bank in their Santiago office.

HOME | ABOUT | BLOG

NICOLA123

About two years ago, my job was getting really boring. I liked the bank and enjoyed working with my coworkers, but I needed a change. I wanted to become a manager because I thought the work would be more interesting and that I would have the chance to travel to different countries.

However, I knew that it was very important for managers in my bank to write and speak excellent Spanish. I studied Spanish in school, but I stopped when I was 16, so I couldn't remember much. I decided to try and improve my Spanish quickly so that I could apply for a job as a manager.

To begin with, I studied my old Spanish textbook from school and did a lot of exercises. After that, I started reading Spanish newspapers online for 30 minutes every day and looked up the meaning of any new words in my dictionary. Soon I could understand nearly everything I read. After a while, I found a website where I could practice listening and speaking. Then, I joined a Spanish class at a language school in my town and went to classes twice a week. In the end, after about 18 months, I could understand and speak Spanish pretty well.

I decided to start applying for management jobs at the bank, and last month I got an offer for a job in Santiago, Chile. My new job starts in September, so I have a few weeks to find an apartment. I'm really excited about going to live in Chile.

2 WRITING SKILLS
Linking: ordering events

a Complete the blog below with the words in the box.

then	the end	after	soon	a while	~~first~~

How I became **a top chef**

Three years ago, I was a terrible cook. I could cook some eggs for my family, but I couldn't cook anything more exciting than that. Two years later, I got a job at a top restaurant in Los Angeles as a chef. Do you want to know how I did it?

At [1] ___first___, my wife helped me. She showed me how to make some simple dishes, such as roast chicken and potatoes and spaghetti bolognese. [2] __________ that, I started going to cooking classes at a school in Chicago, where I learned how to cook a lot of different dishes from all over the world. [3] __________ I started inviting my friends to my house for dinner, and I cooked some of the meals I learned in my classes. After [4] __________, my friends told me I was an amazing cook and that I should become a chef. [5] __________, I entered an important cooking competition on television and, to my surprise, I won! In [6] __________, I got an offer to work at the Ritz Hotel as one of their chefs, so I gave up my office job, and I've never regretted it for one moment.

3 WRITING

a Read the notes and write Sophia's blog about how she changed her trip to work.

Notes for Sophia's blog

2 years ago: go to work by bus = a lot of traffic, 1 hour +
buy a bicycle? but not very fit

bought old bicycle from friend ...
1) frightened of riding a bike on road – so many cars & trucks
2) went to a park – rode slowly, 5–10 mins.
3) house to local stores – 2 km
4) house to downtown – 5 km
5) everywhere on my bike

now: 8 km to work – feel fit & healthy
only 30 mins to work – save 1 hour a day

Reading and listening extension

Remembering the Past

As she celebrates her 100th birthday, Kimi Tanaka talks to *Youth2day* magazine about growing up.

1
My family didn't have much money, but my brothers and I had what we needed. We didn't feel poor. We were like everyone else around here. We used to get together with the other children and play outside every day. We all got along well. It was a nice place to be. Everything used to happen in that street. I met my future husband in the neighborhood. He lived across from us. When we got engaged, we had a party in the street. It was wonderful. It's changed a lot. It's a lot quieter now. The children don't play outside. I know their lives are busier, but I don't think the kids are happier. And they're fatter than we were! I can't believe that so many children are overweight these days.

2
We used to eat three times a day and no more. We had a much healthier diet: a lot of vegetables, some meat, and very little sugar. There didn't use to be junk food like French fries and burgers, and no one needed to go on a diet or get fit. Everyone on our street, children and adults, used to work so hard.

3
It wasn't all better. A lot of people smoked. We didn't know how bad smoking was. My husband was a regular smoker. Fortunately, he gave up smoking when our children were born.

4
My husband used to work in the local car factory. He worked hard but didn't get paid very much. It was difficult sometimes. People are richer and their lives are easier now, especially with the Internet. But our lives were happier then. I wouldn't change my life then for anything.

1 READING

a Read the magazine article. Match the numbered paragraphs 1–4 with the titles a–d.

1 Paragraph 1 — c	a How We Used to Eat
2 Paragraph 2	b Not All About the Money
3 Paragraph 3	c Playing Outside
4 Paragraph 4	d Unknown Dangers

b Read the magazine article again and underline the correct answers.

Kimi thinks …

1 the streets *are* / *used to be* much quieter *now* / *in the past.*
2 the children *are* / *used to be* happier *now* / *in the past.*
3 people *have* / *used to have* healthier diets *now* / *in the past.*
4 more people *smoke* / *used to smoke* *now* / *in the past.*
5 people *are* / *used to be* richer *now* / *in the past.*

c Read the magazine article again and check (✓) the correct answers.

1 Kimi's family …
  a ☐ was very poor.
  b ☐ had better lives than their neighbors.
  c ☑ was similar to the other families where they lived.
2 There was a party in the street …
  a ☐ before Kimi got married.
  b ☐ when Kimi got married.
  c ☐ when Kimi met her husband.
3 People didn't use to go on a diet or need to get fit because …
  a ☐ they didn't like exercising.
  b ☐ they preferred to eat junk food.
  c ☐ they worked so much.
4 People used to smoke a lot because …
  a ☐ it was much cheaper.
  b ☐ they didn't understand it was dangerous.
  c ☐ you could smoke and buy cigarettes everywhere.
5 Kimi thinks …
  a ☐ richer people are happier.
  b ☐ she would prefer to grow up now.
  c ☐ the Internet has made people's lives easier.

d Write about how your life has changed over the past ten years. Write about what you used to do and what you do now. Write about:

- your education
- your free time
- your friends and family.

2 LISTENING

a 07.04 Listen to the conversation. Complete the chart with the names in the box.

Brian Ramirez   Lisa Baker   Martin Dowd
~~Mike Andrews~~   Nick Downes

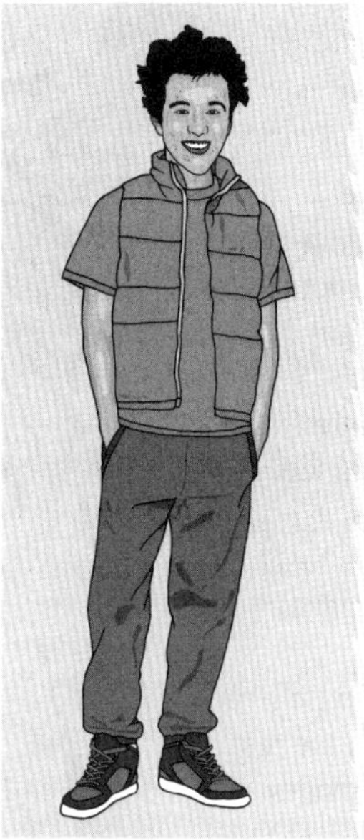

	Name	20 years ago	Now
1	Mike Andrews	poor	rich
2		popular	popular
3		good looking	overweight and unhealthy
4		didn't like someone	is married to the person he didn't like
5		overweight	thin and healthy

b 07.04 Listen to the conversation again and complete the sentences. Write one word in each space.

1 Nick Downes used to be married to Jenny Wang.
2 Jenny wanted Nick to stop ________ and ________ coffee.
3 Lisa Baker has ________ a lot of weight and is a lot ________ than she used to be.
4 Lisa is going to get ________ to a German man.
5 Mike Andrews is a lot ________ than he used to be.
6 Brian Ramirez didn't use to ________ Nicole Aydin.

c Write about your friends and family ten years ago. Remember to include:

- what they used to do
- what they used to look like
- what they used to be like.

Review and extension

1 GRAMMAR

Correct the sentences.

1 Ronaldo is one of most famous soccer players in the world.
Ronaldo is one of the most famous soccer players in the world.
2 I think São Paulo is the most biggest city in Brazil.
3 My brother didn't used to like coffee when he was a teenager.
4 This exercise is more easier than the last one.
5 I'm studying harder this year as last year.
6 San Francisco is the expensivest city in California.

2 VOCABULARY

Correct the sentences.

1 I think you should give out smoking if you want to get fit.
I think you should give up smoking if you want to get fit.
2 You'll have to get a diet if you want to lose weight.
3 My brother has a new job and gets paying very well.
4 She loves her boyfriend, and I think they'll get engage soon.
5 While he was at college, he got to knowing Percem.

3 WORDPOWER *change*

Match 1–8 with a–h to make sentences.

1 [f] The server hasn't given you
2 [ ] OK, let's go and play tennis. You can change
3 [ ] When you go away on vacation, it's better to change
4 [ ] We always go to Florida. Let's go to Mexico
5 [ ] You should keep
6 [ ] To fly from New York to Sydney, you usually have to
7 [ ] She planned to take the train to Atlanta, but at the last minute she changed

a some change in your bag for the bus.
b this summer for a change.
c your money at a bank, not at the airport.
d her mind and flew instead.
e change planes in Dallas or Los Angeles.
f the right change. You gave him $20, not $10.
g into your shorts and tennis shoes in the bathroom.

REVIEW YOUR PROGRESS

Look again at Review Your Progress on p. 76 of the Student's Book. How well can you do these things now?
3 = very well   2 = well   1 = not so well

I CAN ...	
talk about life-changing events	☐
describe health and lifestyle changes	☐
talk to the doctor	☐
write a blog about an achievement.	☐

8A THE PHOTO WAS TAKEN 90 YEARS AGO

1 VOCABULARY Art, music, and literature

a Look at the types of art, music, and literature and label the pictures.

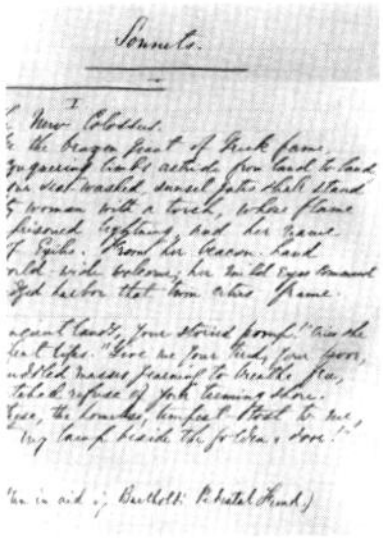

1 poem

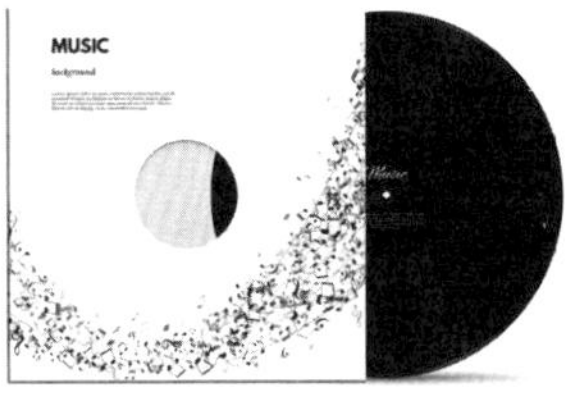

2 ______

3 ______

4 ______

5 ______

6 ______

7 ______

8 ______

b Read the sentences. Which topic is each person talking about, architecture (A), music (M), or literature (L)?

1 [M] "At the age of five, he was already composing songs."
2 [ ] "The best-selling album was recorded in one week."
3 [ ] "The novel was translated into more than 20 languages."
4 [ ] "The Guggenheim Museum is known for its unusual design."
5 [ ] "Two hundred years later, her poetry is still studied in schools."
6 [ ] "The pyramids in Central America were built by the Maya."

2 GRAMMAR The passive: simple present and simple past

a Complete the sentences about the Statue of Liberty. Use the simple present or simple past passive forms of the verbs in parentheses.

The Statue of Liberty [1] is known (know) around the world as a symbol of the United States, but it [2] ______ (not make) there. It [3] ______ (design) in France by Frédéric Auguste Bartholdi. It [4] ______ (give) to the U.S. by the people of France. The statue's head and arm [5] ______ (finish) first. In fact, these parts [6] ______ (make) before the rest of the statue [7] ______ (design). At first, there wasn't enough money to finish the rest of the statue. Finally, enough money [8] ______ (find). Over 120,000 people helped pay for the statue – most of them gave less than $1. The rest of the statue [9] ______ (create) in small pieces in France, and the pieces [10] ______ (take) to the United States by ship. Finally, the statue [11] ______ (put) together in New York. It [12] ______ (finish) in 1886.These days, it [13] ______ (visit) by over 3.2 million tourists every year.

b Rewrite the sentences. Use the passive. Say who does/did the action only if this information is important.

1 They make Porsche cars in Germany.
Porsche cars are made in Germany.
2 They built the Eiffel Tower in 1889.
______
3 George Orwell wrote the novel *Nineteen Eighty-Four* in 1948.
______
4 They held the 2012 Olympic Games in London.
______
5 Steven Spielberg directed the movie *Schindler's List* in 1993.
______
6 They grow the best coffee in Colombia.
______
7 They sold over 17 million new cars in the U.S. in 2018.
______
8 This factory produces 5,000 bicycles every year.
______

8B I'VE BEEN A FAN FOR 20 YEARS

1 GRAMMAR
Present perfect with *for* and *since*

a Complete the exchanges. Use the present perfect forms of the verbs in parentheses and *for* or *since*.

1 **A** Have you always loved (you, love) horses?
B Yes, I ________ (love) horses ________ I was a little girl.

2 **A** ________ (you, live) in Nevada ________ a long time?
B Yes, we ________ (live) here all our lives.

3 **A** How long ________ (you, be) married to Lucy?
B We ________ (be) married ________ 2005, but I ________ (know) her ________ longer.

4 **A** How long ________ (you, have) your stomachache?
B I ________ (have) it ________ last night.

5 **A** How long ________ (you, work) as a journalist?
B I ________ (be) a journalist ________ over 20 years.

b Underline the correct words to complete the sentences.

1 We *'ve lived* / *lived* here for 10 years – from 1964 to 1974.
2 I *know* / *'ve known* Sam since we went to school together.
3 My daughter *'s been* / *was* in the U.S. for six weeks, but she's flying home from San Francisco tomorrow.
4 She *had* / *'s had* a headache since she woke up this morning.
5 I *'ve been* / *was* in Quito since 2012, but before that I *worked* / *'ve worked* in Madrid for two years.
6 John *had* / *'s had* a motorcycle since he was 16 years old.

2 VOCABULARY
Sports and leisure activities

a Which verb do we use to talk about each sport and activity? Complete the chart with the words in the box.

~~gymnastics~~ squash golf surfing yoga volleyball track and field snowboarding ice skating tennis basketball soccer aerobics jogging ice hockey rock climbing karate skateboarding scuba diving windsurfing judo

play	go	do
		gymnastics

b 08.01 Listen and check.

c Complete the crossword puzzle.

→ Across

2 Soccer players have to run fast and kick the ball very hard.
4 Why don't we play ________ when we go to the beach? I have a ball and the nets are already there.
6 The beaches in Maine are often very windy, so they're good for ________.
8 My uncle sometimes goes rock ________ in the mountains.
9 Rafael Nadal is one of the greatest ________ players in the world.
10 When I'm stressed, I do ________. It helps me relax.

↓ Down

1 I think that the most popular sport in Canada is ice ________.
2 I'm not very good at skiing, but I love ________ – it's a lot of fun!
3 My grandparents play ________ twice a week. They play all 18 holes, so it's a good way for them to keep fit.
5 I can't run very fast, but I like ________. Sometimes I run about four or five kilometers.
7 Have you ever been scuba ________ in the ocean? I love seeing all the beautiful fish under the water.

3 PRONUNCIATION Word stress

a 08.02 Listen to the words and check (✓) the stressed syllable in each word.

1 snowboarding
a ☑ snow b ☐ board c ☐ ing
2 windsurfing
a ☐ wind b ☐ surf c ☐ ing
3 jogging
a ☐ jog b ☐ ging
4 gymnastics
a ☐ gym b ☐ nas c ☐ tics
5 ice hockey
a ☐ ice b ☐ hock c ☐ ey

8C EVERYDAY ENGLISH
I'm really sorry I haven't called

1 USEFUL LANGUAGE
Apologies and excuses

a Put the words in the correct order to make sentences.

1 to / to dinner / didn't / but / last week, / I / invite you / feel / I meant / well .
I meant to invite you to dinner last week, but I didn't feel well.

2 your / I couldn't / party yesterday / was / come to / sick / because / I'm sorry / I .
____
____

3 I / you / email / my Wi-Fi / because / working / couldn't / wasn't .
____
____

4 didn't / be late / for / to / was / the train / but / delayed / mean / I / the meeting, .
____
____

5 but / didn't / really sorry / were / I / buy you / I'm / the stores / closed / a present, .
____
____

6 working / I / call you / but / my phone / didn't / last night, / wasn't / I'm sorry .
____
____

7 going to / been / by today, / was / the report / but / finish / I've / I / so busy .
____
____

8 you / meant to / send / your address / I / find / a birthday card, / I couldn't / but .
____
____

b Complete the sentences with the words in the box.

fault	had to	mean	~~sorry~~	couldn't	worry
fine	going to	matter	meant		

1 I'm really *sorry* I didn't call you this morning.
2 I __________ send her any flowers for her birthday.
3 I didn't __________ to be so late.
4 It doesn't __________. It's __________.
5 I was __________ take you to a nice restaurant last night.
6 I __________ to come and visit you when you were in the hospital.
7 Don't __________ about it. It wasn't your __________.
8 We were going to come yesterday, but we __________ visit our grandpa in the hospital.

2 PRONUNCIATION
Tones for continuing or finishing

a 08.03 Listen to the sentences. Check (✓) to show if the tone goes up ↗ or down ↘ at the end.

	↗	↘
1 I meant to send you an email	✓	☐
2 I'm sorry I didn't come to your party	☐	☐
3 I couldn't call you last night	☐	☐
4 I had to stay late at work yesterday	☐	☐
5 Sorry, I didn't mean to make you worry	☐	☐
6 I was going to call you	☐	☐
7 I'm sorry I didn't reply to your message	☐	☐
8 I had to visit my grandma yesterday	☐	☐

b 08.04 Does the speaker have anything more to say? Listen and check.

8D SKILLS FOR WRITING
I couldn't put the book down

1 READING

a Read the review of *Nineteen Eighty-Four* and check (✓) the correct answer.

The reviewer thinks that …

a ☐ the book isn't very interesting.
b ☐ the book is based on a true story.
c ☐ life in Oceania is described very well.
d ☐ the ending isn't very good.

Nineteen Eighty-Four was written by George Orwell in 1948 and is set in the future, in 1984. After a nuclear war, Great Britain has become part of the totalitarian state of Oceania, and everybody is controlled by the Party and its leader, Big Brother.

Although Winston Smith works for the Ministry of Truth, he secretly hates the Party and would like to oppose Big Brother. One day he meets and falls in love with Julia, a woman who also works at the Ministry of Truth and secretly hates Big Brother. However, it is very dangerous for Winston and Julia to have a relationship because love is illegal in Oceania.

Nineteen Eighty-Four is a really exciting novel. It's interesting to read, and it describes the world of Oceania and Big Brother very well, so you can really imagine what life is like in a future totalitarian state after a nuclear war. Winston and Julia are wonderful characters, and their illegal love affair is described very well. You can really understand how they feel.

I couldn't put the book down, and I thought the ending was very smart. I would definitely recommend it. It's the best novel I've read in ages!

b Read the review of *Nineteen Eighty-Four* again. Are the sentences true or false?

1 Big Brother is the leader of Oceania.
2 Everybody knows that Winston hates the Party.
3 The reviewer thinks that the story is a little boring.
4 The reviewer thinks the descriptions of people's lives in 1984 are very good.
5 The reviewer thinks *Nineteen Eighty-Four* is a book other people should read.

2 WRITING SKILLS
Positive and negative comments; Linking: *although*, *however*

a Complete the sentences with *although* or *however*.

1 Although I enjoyed the novel, the story is pretty complicated.
2 The descriptions of London during the war were so realistic. ________, sometimes they were a little long and dull.
3 The story was pretty exciting, ________ the book was too long for me to finish on vacation.
4 The characters were described very well. ________, there are so many of them that sometimes I forgot who they were.
5 ________ the ending was kind of sad, I really enjoyed the book and would definitely recommend it.
6 It's an amazing book, ________ the story is sometimes a little hard to follow.

3 WRITING

a Choose one of the following:

1 Write a review of a book you've read. Describe the characters, the descriptions, and the story and give your opinion of the book.
2 Read the notes below and write a review of the children's novel, *War Horse*, by Michael Morpurgo.

Notes for book review
Book: *War Horse*
Author: Michael Morpurgo
Story summary:
- about horse named Joey, sold to British Army at beginning of World War I
- sent to France, ridden by Captain Nicholls
- Captain Nicholls killed in fighting, so Joey given to a younger soldier, Warren
- J becomes friends with another horse, Topthorn: a lot of adventures
- later, J and T taken by Germans
- T killed, but J works for German army until end of war

Review:
- *War Horse* written for children, but really enjoyed it
- story: really interesting
- characters: described really well
- can imagine what WWI was like
- beautiful story, but really sad: made me cry
- happy ending: at end of war J returned to Albert (his original owner before J was sold to army)
- couldn't put it down – definitely recommend …

UNIT 8
Reading and listening extension

1 READING

a Read the article from a tourist brochure. Are the sentences true or false?

1 The Brighton Festival is for people who like reading, listening to music, seeing movies and plays.
2 It is very easy to see an event in the festival.
3 Sam Lee writes most of the songs that he sings.
4 You can see Kaarina Kaikkonen's *Time Passing By* in an art gallery.
5 *Flathampton* is a town in a theater.

b Read the article again and complete the chart to show the correct events for the sentences. Sometimes there is more than one possible answer.

	To Sleep To Dream	Sam Lee	Kaarina Kaikkonen	*Flathampton*
1 This event is outside.			✓	
2 You can listen to music from the past.				
3 There is nothing to see at this event.				
4 The audience must help the actors.				
5 This event tells a story.				

c Read the article again. Check (✓) the correct answers.

1 The Brighton Festival …
a ☐ is a big party that happens on Brighton beach every May.
b ☑ happens in many places in the city, and people often have to join in.
c ☐ happens in people's houses and is not for visitors to the city.

2 In *To Sleep To Dream*, …
a ☐ the audience must listen very carefully.
b ☐ the audience watches a movie about music.
c ☐ the actors can't see the audience.

3 The songs that Sam Lee sings …
a ☐ were written while he was traveling around Britain.
b ☐ were written by the musicians in his band.
c ☐ were found while he was traveling around Britain.

4 *Time Passing By* …
a ☐ is a painting of a clock in Brighton.
b ☐ is made using things belonging to other people.
c ☐ is a sculpture made of clocks.

5 *Flathampton* …
a ☐ is a play where the audience helps build a town.
b ☐ takes place in the town center.
c ☐ is a play about children living in a theater.

d Write a paragraph about a festival that happens near where you live. Remember to include:

- what it is
- where it is
- what happens
- what you like and dislike about it.

THE BRIGHTON FESTIVAL

If you like music; going to art galleries, the movies, or the theater; or learning about books, then you really should visit the Brighton Festival. It has been going since 1965 and is now one of the largest arts festivals in England.

Come to Brighton in May and it's impossible not to see events – such as plays, concerts, movies, dance performances, and exhibitions – take place across the city in theaters, galleries, the street, on the beach, and even in people's own houses.

There have been some amazing events. Here are some of the highlights from the last two years:

Sam Lee is a singer who has spent many years traveling around Britain to find and listen to very old British songs. Many of the songs were written hundreds of years ago, and he performs them with an interesting band of musicians.

Kaarina Kaikkonen is a Finnish artist who often uses other people's clothes to make large sculptures. In *Time Passing By*, the 23-meter-high Clock Tower in the city center was covered in clothes. It was very popular with visitors and artists.

In *To Sleep To Dream*, which was written by Daniel Clark, everyone in the audience wears a blindfold (something that covers the eyes so you can't see) to help them concentrate on the story, which is told with special 3D sound effects and music. In this movie for the ears, your ears become your eyes.

Flathampton is a play with a difference. The whole theater is turned into a town, and the audience is taken through the town by the actors. As the story is told, the audience has to help make the buildings in the town that the actors perform in. It's been extremely popular with children and adults alike.

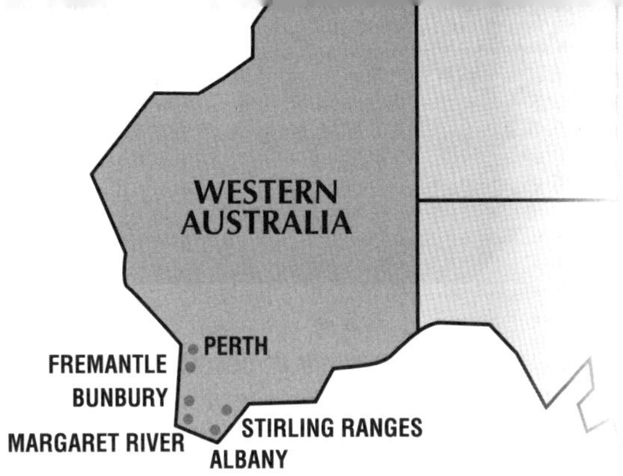

2 LISTENING

a 08.05 Listen to the conversation and look at the map of western Australia. Complete the chart to show where the activities are. Sometimes there is more than one possible answer.

	Stirling Ranges	Perth	Near Fremantle	Bunbury	Margaret River
1 This is for people who enjoy watching foreign movies.		✓			
2 This is not for beginners.					
3 This is for people who don't mind getting wet.					
4 A lot of people will do this on Sunday morning.					
5 A group of young people will perform on a beach.					
6 This is for people who like sports.					

b 08.05 Listen to the conversation again. Underline the correct words to complete the sentences.

1 If you want to know where to go rock climbing at the Stirling Ranges, you can *look on the website* / *visit the information center* / *visit your local bookstore or library*.
2 *The ocean* / *The day* / *The river* affects where Margaret River Surfers meet.
3 The photographs in the art gallery in Perth were taken by *photographers* / *movie directors* / *actors*.
4 On the beach at Wilson Park, you can *listen to* / *write* / *read* poems by young poets.
5 *Jenny* / *Matt* / *Carolina* is going to be doing something active with a large group this weekend.

c Write about your hobbies. Remember to include:

- what you like doing
- how long you've been doing this
- where you do this
- who you do it with.

Review and extension

1 GRAMMAR

Correct the sentences.

1 The Harry Potter stories weren't written of Charles Dickens.
The Harry Potter stories weren't written by Charles Dickens.
2 I knew Veronica since I was a child.
3 We've lived in Guayaquil since more than ten years.
4 St. Paul's Cathedral is designed by Christopher Wren.
5 I have taught at that university from 2016 to 2019.
6 I have played golf from I was 12 years old.

2 VOCABULARY

Correct the sentences.

1 This morning we played volley at the beach.
This morning we played volleyball at the beach.
2 Skateboard is a great way for children to get fit.
3 Do you have a fotograph of your girlfriend?
4 Let's play golfing this afternoon.
5 These days, ice skate is popular in New York City during the winter.
6 When I was in school, I had to do gymnastic every Wednesday.
7 The *Mona Lisa* is one of the most famous paints in the world.
8 Let's do surfing at the beach this afternoon.

3 WORDPOWER *by*

Complete the sentences with the words in the box.

bus next Monday hand mistake heart
~~the library~~ far the way

1 She's waiting for you by *the library*.
2 By __________, are you doing anything on Friday?
3 Sorry, I clicked SEND by __________ before I finished writing the email.
4 I usually come to work by __________.
5 Actors have to learn their lines by __________.
6 These shoes were made by __________. That's why they're more expensive.
7 Usain Bolt is by __________ the best 100-meter runner of the past 15 years.
8 Please send me your report by __________.

REVIEW YOUR PROGRESS

Look again at Review Your Progress on p. 86 of the Student's Book. How well can you do these things now?
3 = very well 2 = well 1 = not so well

I CAN ...	
talk about art, music, and literature	☐
talk about sports and leisure activities	☐
apologize and make and accept excuses	☐
write a book review.	☐

9A IF I DON'T PASS THIS EXAM, I WON'T BE VERY HAPPY

1 VOCABULARY College majors; Education collocations

a Complete the crossword puzzle.

→ Across

5 If you study l*aw* in college, you will learn everything about our legal system.

6 If you want to become a manager in a large company, you should get a degree in business a__________.

7 She's getting a degree in e__________ because she wants to become a teacher.

↓ Down

1 He was really interested in other people and how they think, so he decided to study p__________.

2 He went to college to study d__________ and then got a job as an actor.

3 She studied e__________ in college, and now she's helping design a new bridge across the Ohio River.

4 If you want to become a doctor, you'll have to study m__________ in college.

8 He got a degree in a__________, and now he does beautiful drawings for children's books.

b Complete the sentences with the words in the box.

degree	get	notes	pass	study	accepted
fail	essays	~~grades~~	handed		

1 He got really bad *grades* on his exams, so he's going to repeat the year.

2 She got a college __________ in French and Spanish, and now she works as a tour guide.

3 I have to write three __________ before the end of the year, and each one is 4,000 words long.

4 If she doesn't work hard this semester, I think she might __________ her exams.

5 I have to __________ for an important exam, so I won't go out today or tomorrow.

6 Because he __________ in his essay two days late, he got a grade of only 45%.

7 I didn't take a pen and paper with me to the meeting, but I took some __________ on my phone.

8 He did extremely well on his exams and got __________ to Harvard University.

9 Your daughter has always worked hard, so she'll definitely __________ into college.

10 You should study several hours each day if you want to __________ your exams.

2 GRAMMAR Future real conditionals

a Put the words in the correct order to make sentences.

1 it / tomorrow, / we're / If / to / go skiing / going / snows .
If it snows tomorrow, we're going to go skiing.

2 if / I'll / Canada / to / can / on vacation / I / a / cheap flight / find / go .
____

3 might / they / every day, / study / they / their exams / If / pass .
____

4 to / If / her exams, / might / accepted / she / on / Northwestern University / she / does well / get .
____

5 medicine / have to / excellent grades / get / if / She'll / to study / wants / in college / she .
____

6 call / tonight / tomorrow morning / him / if / doesn't / to / my email / I'll / reply / he .
____

7 on time / give / don't / you / bad grade / if / might / hand in / a / you / essay / Your teacher / your .
____

8 fail / college / your exams, / you / you / If / get into / won't .
____

3 PRONUNCIATION Word groups

a 09.01 Listen to the sentences and mark // where there is a pause.

1 I enjoy studying math in school, // but I hate taking exams.

2 If you take notes in class, it will be easier to study for the exam.

3 I'm going to work harder next year, so that I get better grades.

4 If she fails her exam, she'll have to take it again in January.

5 Although he got excellent grades, he didn't get accepted to Oxford University.

9B I MANAGED TO STOP FEELING SHY

1 GRAMMAR Verb patterns

a Underline the correct words to complete the sentences.

1 I usually finish *to play* / *playing* / *play* tennis at about nine o'clock.
2 We decided *not taking* / *not to take* / *to not take* the next train to Rome.
3 He keeps *to try* / *try* / *trying* to learn Portuguese, but he always gives up.
4 We wanted *see* / *to see* / *seeing* the movie, but there were no tickets left.
5 She promised *to not fail* / *not failing* / *not to fail* any exams this year.
6 I don't mind *not to take* / *to not take* / *not taking* a vacation this year, if we can take one next year.
7 They learned *to speak* / *speaking* / *speak* English by talking to their grandfather.
8 I hope *go* / *to go* / *going* on vacation to Puerto Rico next summer.
9 I really enjoy *to spend* / *spend* / *spending* time with my family.
10 I worry about *to not do* / *not do* / *not doing* well on the exams, but I always pass.

b Complete the sentences with the correct forms of the verbs in the box.

meet get go take snow ~~buy~~ read play

1 He promised _to buy_ her a new phone if she got good grades on her exams.
2 We decided __________ the bus because the train was a lot more expensive.
3 I really enjoy __________ to the theater when I'm in London.
4 She expected __________ a good result, but she didn't.
5 My sisters and I used to love __________ games on the beach when we were little.
6 She's arranged __________ him at the check-in desk at the airport.
7 He finished __________ his book and then went to bed.
8 It started __________ heavily last night, and now they've closed the airport.

2 VOCABULARY Verbs followed by infinitive / verb + *-ing*

a Complete the sentences with the words in the box.

forgot avoid regretted seemed agreed managed ~~arranged~~ recommended disliked missed refused imagined

1 They _arranged_ to meet their friends outside the movie theater at 7:30.
2 When we asked the tour guide, he __________ taking a taxi to the beach.
3 Because she was shy, she __________ meeting new people at parties.
4 She __________ to take her wallet to the restaurant, so her boyfriend had to pay the check.
5 Fortunately, the taxi driver __________ to drive us to the airport when we offered him 50 dollars.
6 He __________ buying a house by the ocean. He thought it would be wonderful to walk on the beach every day.
7 After she moved from the U.S. to Mexico, she really __________ seeing her family in the summer.
8 I went to work early this morning because I wanted to __________ driving downtown during rush hour.
9 Most of the hotels were full, but in the end we __________ to find a beautiful hotel near the beach.
10 When she got bad grades on her exams, she __________ not working harder.
11 The hotel receptionist __________ to understand what I was saying because she brought some sandwiches to our room five minutes later.
12 He __________ to leave the waiter a tip because the service was so slow.

b Underline the correct words to complete the sentences.

1 She has *avoided* / *agreed* / *missed* to meet Luke for coffee after work.
2 He usually *avoids* / *missed* / *recommends* speaking to his neighbors because he's pretty shy.
3 Let's *refuse* / *forget* / *arrange* to have dinner together one night this week.
4 I'm sorry, but I *managed* / *forgot* / *refused* to get any bread when I was at the supermarket.
5 She *regrets* / *avoids* / *recommends* going to the Alhambra palace in Granada. She says it's beautiful.
6 Now that you live in an apartment, do you *miss* / *regret* / *imagine* having a yard?
7 I don't want to go to the party, so if they ask me to go with them, I will politely *forget* / *manage* / *refuse*.
8 She *imagined* / *disliked* / *recommended* swimming in the ocean because the water was always so cold.
9 Our baby *seems* / *manages* / *refuses* to prefer classical music to pop music.
10 Did you *refuse* / *manage* / *seem* to get some tickets to the concert? They almost sold out on the first day.

9C EVERYDAY ENGLISH
Who's calling, please?

1 USEFUL LANGUAGE Calling people you know; Calling people you don't know

a Put the conversation in the correct order.

A Is it possible to speak to Becky Yu, please?
B Of course. I'll transfer you to her office.

[ ] **C** Does she have your number?
[ ] **C** OK. Would you like her to call you back?
[ ] **C** No, I'm afraid she's not available. She's in a meeting. Can I take a message?
[ ] **A** Oh, hello. Is Becky there, please?
[ ] **C** Yes, of course. Who's calling, please?
[ ] **A** Yes, OK. Can you tell her that I called?
[ ] **A** Yes, please. I'm here all morning.
[1] **C** Hello, Becky Yu's office.
[ ] **A** This is Paul Roberts speaking.
[ ] **A** Yes, she does.

C Great. I'll ask her to call you back.
A Thanks. Bye.

b 09.02 Listen and check.

c Complete the conversation with the words in the box.

need to go   I have   ~~is this~~   it's   just saying   soon
catch that   call you back   call   good time   it is

AMY Oh, hello, 1 is this Rob?
ROB Yes, 2 ________.
AMY Hi, 3 ________ Amy.
ROB Oh, hi, Amy.
AMY Is now a 4 ________ to talk?
ROB Well, I'm a little busy.
AMY Sorry, Rob, I didn't 5 ________.
ROB Yes, I was 6 ________ that I'm busy. Sorry, but 7 ________ a meeting in five minutes. Can I 8 ________?
AMY Sure. Is everything OK?
ROB Yes, everything's fine, but I 9 ________.
AMY OK. 10 ________ me when you have time.
ROB Talk to you 11 ________. Bye.
AMY Bye.

d 09.03 Listen and check.

2 PRONUNCIATION
Main stress: contrastive

a 09.04 We can use contrastive stress to correct something someone else has said. Listen to the pairs of sentences. In each pair, check (✓) the sentence where you hear a strong stress.

1 a [ ] The movie starts at 8:50.
  b [✓] The movie starts at 8:15.
2 a [ ] We're catching the nine o'clock bus.
  b [ ] We're catching the ten o'clock bus.
3 a [ ] My new boyfriend's name is James.
  b [ ] My new boyfriend's name is John.
4 a [ ] The show is on channel 11.
  b [ ] The show is on channel 7.
5 a [ ] We're leaving for vacation on Tuesday.
  b [ ] We're leaving for vacation on Thursday.
6 a [ ] I was born in 1990.
  b [ ] I was born in 1991.

9D SKILLS FOR WRITING
Online learning is new to me

1 READING

a Read the profile of a French student and check (✓) the correct answer.

a ☐ Claude's studying French.
b ☐ Claude's going to study in the U.S. next year.
c ☐ The online course is about American movies.
d ☐ Claude works in a café every day.

b Read Claude's profile again. Are the sentences true or false?

1 Claude likes his major in college.
2 He already speaks and writes English very well.
3 He hopes he will be better at writing in English after the course.
4 He wants to make friends with American students.
5 He doesn't often go to see movies with his friends in Paris.

TELL US ABOUT YOU ...

Hi, everyone. My name's Claude, and I'm French. I'm doing an English and German major at Sorbonne University here in Paris. I'm really enjoying it. At the moment, I'm studying 20th-century American novelists, such as Ernest Hemingway. It's really interesting, but the best thing about my degree is that next year I'll spend six months in the U.K. and six months in Germany – I can't wait! I also get the chance to take an online course in film studies. I can already speak English very well because my father's American. However, my written English isn't very good.

HOW DO YOU FEEL ABOUT THIS ONLINE COURSE?

I've always loved movies, so I'm really looking forward to taking this American film studies course. I hope it will help me understand American movies better and improve my written English at the same time. I'm also very excited about making friends with students from different countries.

WHAT DO YOU DO WHEN YOU'RE NOT STUDYING?

I have a part-time job in a café near the Arc de Triomphe, in the heart of Paris. I work there three evenings a week and sometimes on Sundays, too. In my free time, I like going out with my friends. We usually go to the movies, or sometimes we have dinner at one of the cheap restaurants in the Latin Quarter.

2 WRITING SKILLS Avoiding repetition

a Change the words in **bold** in the sentences to pronouns.

1 I'm getting a degree in medicine. I'm really enjoying **my degree** ___it___.
2 The other students in my class all come from different countries. **The other students** ______ all speak English very well.
3 My cousin Paola is also studying at the same university as me. **Paola's** ______ getting a degree in business administration.
4 When I'm not studying, I spend time with my girlfriend, Anna. I see **Anna** ______ three or four times a week.
5 We haven't decided which hotel to stay at when we go to Rome. I think we should try and find **a hotel** ______ near the Colosseum.
6 My dad's an IT consultant. **My dad** ______ usually works from home, but sometimes **my dad** ______ has to go to Oakland for meetings.
7 My brother and I are both studying law. My parents have always wanted **my brother and I** ______ to become lawyers, just like my father.
8 I have a part-time job working in a supermarket. **This part-time job** ______ isn't very interesting, but I do **this part-time job** ______ because I need the money.

3 WRITING

a Read the notes and write a student profile for Hitomi, who is also taking the online American film studies class.

Student profile – notes

Tell us about you ...

- Hitomi: from Osaka, Japan
- master's degree in economics – Tokyo University
- next year: job in London or New York?
- studied English at school: writing OK, but speaking???

How do you feel about this online course?

- want to learn about Am. movies: always loved Am. movies
- improve English?
- talk about movies with other students?
- my English: improve quickly?

What do you do when you're not studying?

sports – tennis x1 or x2 a week
– golf on weekends
– gym at the university: like keeping fit
– yoga when stressed: helps me relax

Reading and listening extension

1 READING

a Read the text. Complete the sentences with the subjects in the box.

~~engineering~~	law	medicine	psychology

1 More foreign students study _engineering_ than any other subject.
2 Li Jing is getting a degree in ________.
3 Luis is studying ________.
4 Andreas is studying ________.

b Read the text again. Check (✓) the correct answers.

1 The country with the most foreign students studying at its universities is …
   a ☐ China.
   b ☐ the U.K.
   c ☑ the U.S.
2 According to the Migration Policy Institute, the number of foreign students studying in the U.S. in the 1950s was …
   a ☐ half the number of students in the 1960s.
   b ☐ 1.1 million.
   c ☐ the same as in the 1950s.
3 Li Jing wanted to come to the U.S. …
   a ☐ a long time ago.
   b ☐ to study English.
   c ☐ to find a job.
4 Luis decided to go to the U.S. because …
   a ☐ he went to school there.
   b ☐ he knows the country well.
   c ☐ he wanted to study law.
5 How does Andreas feel about being in Chicago?
   a ☐ He would like to be somewhere else.
   b ☐ He would like to stay here longer.
   c ☐ He prefers the food in Germany.

c Read the text again and complete the sentences.

1 If Luis doesn't pass his _exams_, he will have to repeat his classes.
2 Li Jing imagined going to ________ for a long time.
3 Andreas went to the U.S. because he ________ English.
4 Li Jing has recommended ________ in Los Angeles to a friend of hers.
5 Andreas will try to find ________ here if he does well on his final exams.

d Write a paragraph about your experiences studying. Remember to include:

- what you've studied
- where you've studied
- which exams you've taken
- what you like and dislike about studying.

Studying in the U.S.

About 1.1 million foreign students go to college in the U.S., with the largest number, over 350,000, coming from China. The U.S. is the most popular country for foreign students, with the U.K. and China as the second and third most popular destinations.

The most popular majors for these students are engineering and business administration. Approximately 21% of foreign students are engineering majors, while 19% are business administration majors.

A recent report by the Migration Policy Institute (a North American and European organization focused on improving immigration policies) shows that the number of foreign students at U.S. universities has doubled every decade since the 1950s. It reached a record high of 1.1 million in the 2016–17 academic year. So, what makes the U.S. such an attractive place to study?

Li Jing, 19, Hong Kong
I decided to study in the U.S. because I love reading American authors, and I've always dreamed about coming here. I applied to five universities in the U.S. and got accepted to UCLA in California to study medicine. I'm really happy with my classes, and I've met a lot of students from all over the world. Los Angeles is a fun city, and I've already told my friend who would like to study abroad next year how great it is.

Luis, 20, Ecuador
I studied at an international school in Quito, and I've been to the U.S. many times. I have family in New York City, so it seemed to be a good choice for me. I'm studying law. I have to write a lot of essays. At the end of the year, I need to hand in three long essays and also pass my exams. I hope I manage to do everything. Failing the exams means repeating the year. I don't want to do that!

Andreas, 23, Germany
I wanted to study abroad, and because English is the only foreign language I speak, I decided to come here. I'm happy I came to Chicago. The weather is similar to my hometown in Germany, but the culture and the food are different. The city is beautiful, and the people are really friendly. I'm studying for my final exams in psychology right now. If I pass, I might stay here and look for a job.

Review and extension

1 GRAMMAR

Correct the sentences.

1 If I'll work hard, I'll pass the exam.
  If I work hard, I'll pass the exam.
2 I want that you buy me some bread and milk from the store.
3 We won't play golf this afternoon if it will rain.
4 She enjoys to read books about dinosaurs.
5 Will you go to college next year if you'll get good grades?
6 I just finished to have dinner with my family.

2 VOCABULARY

Correct the sentences.

1 When Robert left Indiana to go and live in Australia, he regretted seeing his friends from home.
  When Robert left Indiana to go and live in Australia, he missed seeing his friends from home.
2 He did well really at school and got into a good college.
3 She got a very bad note on her last history essay.
4 Although they worked hard, they both fell their math exams.
5 She always took taxis because she misliked waiting for buses.
6 He made a degree in medicine, and now he's a doctor.

3 WORDPOWER Multi-word verbs with *put*

Complete the sentences with the prepositions in the box.

on down away off ~~back~~

1 Please put the milk __back__ in the fridge when you're finished with it.
2 They'll put ________ their notes after they finish studying.
3 OK, everybody. The exam is finished now, so please put your pens ________ and stop writing. Thank you.
4 It's raining pretty hard now. Why don't we put ________ our game of tennis until tomorrow?
5 I usually put ________ a suit when I go on a job interview.

2 LISTENING

a 09.05 Listen to the conversation. Are the sentences true or false?

1 Roberto has written six essays this semester.
2 Roberto is in his first year of college.
3 Roberto was late for class for two weeks.
4 Roberto failed his exams.
5 Roberto studies for the exam every Wednesday.
6 There are 25 students studying psychology in Roberto's year.

b 09.05 Listen to the conversation again. Match 1–6 with a–f to make sentences.

1 [b] The professor isn't going to grade Roberto's essay if
2 [ ] If Roberto doesn't come to class,
3 [ ] Roberto didn't go to some classes because
4 [ ] Roberto might not pass the exam if
5 [ ] Roberto might not be in the psychology program next year if
6 [ ] The professor is not happy with Roberto because

a he doesn't go to every class.
b he doesn't hand it in on time.
c he fails the exam.
d he hasn't read any of the books.
e he was sick.
f he won't learn anything.

c Write about how you study for an exam. Remember to include:

- how long you spend studying
- what you do to help remember information
- how good you are at taking exams.

REVIEW YOUR PROGRESS

Look again at Review Your Progress on p. 96 of the Student's Book. How well can you do these things now?
3 = very well 2 = well 1 = not so well

I CAN ...	
talk about future possibilities	☐
describe actions and feelings	☐
make telephone calls	☐
write a personal profile.	☐

10A WOULD YOU DO THE RIGHT THING?

1 GRAMMAR Present and future unreal conditionals

a Put the words in the correct order to make sentences.

1 I / to the police station / If / take it / found some money / in the street, / I'd .
If I found some money in the street, I'd take it to the police station.

2 complain / the server / you / with your check / Would / if / made a mistake ?
____

3 would / at school / there were / do / What / if / no teachers / you ?
____

4 I / I could / on gas / rode my bike to work, / a lot of money / If / save .
____

5 did yoga / I / feel / every day / less stressed / I / would / if .
____

6 take a taxi / If / the last bus, / I'd /missed / have to / I .
____

7 if / I / could stop / became rich / working / I .
____

8 you / would / the movie / download it / you / on the Internet, / found / If ?
____

b Underline the correct words to make present and future unreal conditional sentences.

1 If I *would be* / *were* / *am* you, I *will buy* / *bought* / *would buy* her some flowers.
2 *Could you work* / *Will you work* / *Did you work* seven days a week if you *need* / *needed* / *would need* the money?
3 If the store assistant *would be* / *were* / *will be* rude to me, *I'm complaining* / *I complained* / *I'd complain* to the manager.
4 *I could take* / *I'll take* / *I took* you to the bus station if my car *isn't* / *weren't* / *wouldn't be* at the garage.
5 If you *will walk* / *would walk* / *walked* five kilometers every day, *you feel* / *you felt* / *you'd feel* much healthier.
6 If my new watch *stopped* / *will stop* / *would stop* working after two weeks, I *'ll take* / *'d take* / *take* it back to the store.
7 I *didn't walk* / *wouldn't walk* / *won't walk* home by myself if I *am* / *would be* / *were* you.
8 What *did you do* / *do you do* / *would you do* if you *lost* / *would lose* / *will lose* your car keys?

2 VOCABULARY Multi-word verbs

a Match 1–8 with a–h to make sentences.

1 [h] Could you pass
2 [ ] Why don't you come
3 [ ] At some hotels, you have to hand
4 [ ] My neighbor joined
5 [ ] Because they were very tired, they didn't feel
6 [ ] I asked him to speak in English, but he kept
7 [ ] His mother took
8 [ ] He was offered a great job, but he turned it

a down because he didn't want to leave Italy.
b care of him when he was sick last week.
c in our game of volleyball.
d in your passport when you first arrive.
e on speaking in German, so I couldn't understand him.
f like going to the movies, so they watched a movie on TV.
g over to my house for dinner on Saturday?
h on my complaint to the manager, please?

b Underline the correct words to complete the sentences.

1 It's very rude to keep *in* / *on* / *after* talking when the movie starts.
2 When Jack lost his job, they decided to put *up* / *on* / *off* their wedding until he could find another one.
3 My neighbor came *over* / *after* / *to* for a cup of coffee this morning.
4 If you don't feel *down* / *like* / *off* eating much, just have some fruit.
5 My sister's sad because she and her boyfriend broke *down* / *off* / *up* yesterday.
6 I found someone's cell phone under my desk, so I handed it *in* / *on* / *up* to my teacher.
7 Who's going to take care *up* / *for* / *of* your grandpa while your grandma's away?
8 Can you pass *up* / *on* / *in* my message to Mr. Henderson when he gets back on Monday, please?

3 PRONUNCIATION Sentence stress: vowel sounds

a 10.01 Listen to the sentences and check (✓) to show if the words in **bold** are stressed or unstressed.

	Stressed	Unstressed
1 If I had a lot of money, I **would** buy an expensive sports car.	[ ]	[✓]
2 **Would** you marry him if he didn't live so far away?	[ ]	[ ]
3 If I were you, I **wouldn't** go swimming in the ocean today.	[ ]	[ ]
4 If he asked her to go to Argentina with him, she probably **would**.	[ ]	[ ]
5 I **would** come and stay with you in New York if the flights weren't so expensive.	[ ]	[ ]
6 She **wouldn't** have to drive to work every day if she lived closer to her office.	[ ]	[ ]

10B I'M TOO EMBARRASSED TO COMPLAIN

1 GRAMMAR Quantifiers; *too / not enough*

a Underline the correct words to complete the conversation.

A We'll need [1]*much / a lot of / any* flour, sugar, and, of course, carrots to make this cake. We'll also need [2]*a little / many / a few* orange juice.
B Well, there's [3]*any / no / many* flour in the cupboard, so I'll have to go and buy some.
A Good idea. So, what else do we need? Um, butter … how [4]*many / few / much* butter do we have in the fridge?
B Um, we don't have [5]*many / much / some* butter. Just one stick – eight ounces.
A OK, that's fine. And what about eggs – how [6]*many / much / any* eggs are there?
B There aren't [7]*much / many / any* eggs – only four.
A OK. And do we have [8]*much / a little / any* carrots?
B Yes, I think we have [9]*a few / much / few* carrots, maybe three or four. Let me just check … oh, actually, there aren't [10]*any / many / much* carrots. I think I ate the last one yesterday. Sorry!
A Never mind. OK, so can you also get me [11]*any / some / a little* carrots from the supermarket, please?
B OK, you'd better make me a shopping list …

b Underline the correct words to complete the sentences.

1 I couldn't take a shower this morning because the water wasn't *enough warm / warm enough*.
2 There's *too much / too many* sugar in my coffee now – it's disgusting!
3 I'm sorry, I don't have *enough milk / milk enough* to make coffee for everyone.
4 You're driving *too much / too* slowly – we won't get to the airport on time!
5 You aren't speaking *enough clearly / clearly enough*. I can't understand you.
6 There are *too many / too much* cars in the city these days. The traffic's always terrible!
7 You're walking *too much quickly / too quickly* for me. I can't walk as fast as you.
8 My apartment isn't *enough big / big enough* to have a birthday party for all my friends.

2 VOCABULARY Noun formation

a Complete the crossword puzzle.

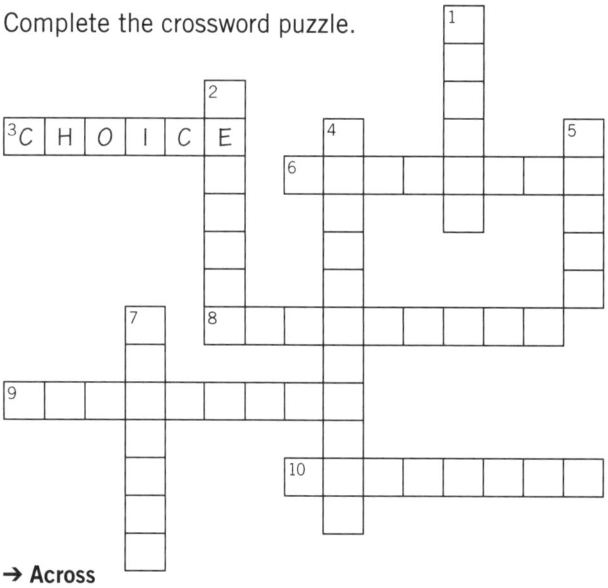

→ Across

3 There isn't much c*hoice* in the little supermarket near my house. For example, they only have two types of bread.
6 The directors made the d_________ to sell the company.
8 I buy books online. They're usually d_________ to my house within three or four days.
9 Excuse me. I'd like to make a formal c_________ about the quality of the food in this hotel.
10 I think people should always c_________ in a restaurant if the service is bad.

↓ Down

1 So you've ordered a new phone. What color did you c_________ – black or white?
2 I've d_________ to redecorate my kitchen, so I just went to the store to buy some paint.
4 Our hotel was really horrible. It didn't match the d_________ they gave on their website.
5 Did you e_________ the new Disney movie?
7 Why has the flight to Rio de Janeiro been delayed by five hours? Can you e_________ that to me?

3 PRONUNCIATION Word stress

a Check (✓) the correct stress marking for each word.

1 decision
a ☑ decision
b ☐ decision
2 enjoyment
a ☐ enjoyment
b ☐ enjoyment
3 complaint
a ☐ complaint
b ☐ complaint
4 description
a ☐ description
b ☐ description
5 explanation
a ☐ explanation
b ☐ explanation
6 delivery
a ☐ delivery
b ☐ delivery
7 describe
a ☐ describe
b ☐ describe
8 complain
a ☐ complain
b ☐ complain

b 10.02 Listen and check.

10C EVERYDAY ENGLISH
Can I exchange it for something else?

1 USEFUL LANGUAGE Returning goods and making complaints

a Put the conversation in the correct order.

CUSTOMER Good morning. Could you help me, please?
SALES ASSISTANT Yes, of course. How can I help?

☐ CUSTOMER Could I speak to the manager, please?
1 CUSTOMER I'd like to return this speaker, please.
☐ SALES ASSISTANT Do you have a receipt?
☐ SALES ASSISTANT Would you like to exchange it for something else?
☐ SALES ASSISTANT Well, I'm terribly sorry, but we don't give refunds without a receipt.
☐ CUSTOMER No, I'm sorry, I don't. It was a present from my boyfriend, but the sound quality is very bad.
☐ SALES ASSISTANT Yes, of course. I'll go and get him.
☐ CUSTOMER No, I'd just like a refund, please.

MANAGER What seems to be the problem?
CUSTOMER I'd like to make a complaint.

b 10.03 Listen and check.

c Put the words in the correct order to make sentences.

1 but / excuse me, / ordered / isn't / what / this / I .
Excuse me, but this isn't what I ordered.
2 ask / right away / I'll / that for / you / someone / to look at .
______
3 been here / still haven't / ordered / we've / but / for over an hour, / we .
______
4 they're / because / small / don't / these shoes / me / fit / a little .
______
5 mind, / I've / my / I've decided / keep it / changed / and / to .
______
6 to / I'd / for / exchange it / something else / like .
______
7 please / I'd / to / this watch, / return / like .
______
8 full refund / a / give / I'll / you .
______
9 hasn't been / helpful / sales assistant / your / very .
______

d 10.04 Listen and check.

2 PRONUNCIATION Sentence stress

a 10.05 Listen and decide where the main stress is in each question. Check (✓) the stressed word.

1 Can you bring us the check, please?
a ☐ Can b ☑ check
2 Would you like me to give you a refund?
a ☐ like b ☐ give
3 Did you bring your receipt with you?
a ☐ bring b ☐ receipt
4 Where did you buy it?
a ☐ Where b ☐ buy
5 Could you wait a moment, please?
a ☐ Could b ☐ wait
6 Can you take our order now, please?
a ☐ take b ☐ order
7 Can I exchange these jeans for another pair?
a ☐ Can b ☐ exchange
8 Could you call the manager, please?
a ☐ call b ☐ manager

10D SKILLS FOR WRITING

We're really sorry we missed it

1 READING

a Read the three emails and check (✓) the correct answers.

	Email A	Email B	Email C
1 Which email is about changing the date of a meeting?	☐	☐	☐
2 Which email is about some problems with a family vacation?	☐	☐	☐
3 Which email is from the parents of a very young child who was sick?	☐	☐	☐

Email A

Dear Mr. Patterson,

Thank you for your email of September 5 about the problems you had on your vacation with Turkish Sun Tours. I am writing to apologize for putting you in a different hotel from your friends. Unfortunately, our agents in Turkey made a mistake with your booking and did not reserve enough rooms at Hotel Paradise. This is why they had to put your family in another hotel in the same resort.

I hope you will book a vacation with us again in the future, and we would like to offer you a 25% discount on your next vacation with us. This is our way of apologizing for the problems you had.

Sincerely,

Sam Polat

Customer Services Manager, Turkish Sun Tours

Email B

Hi Jim,

Just a quick message to say I'm sorry that we couldn't come to your house for dinner last Saturday. Unfortunately, our youngest son, Jack, had a really high temperature, so we couldn't leave him with our babysitter.

Some friends of ours are coming over for lunch next Sunday, so, if you're free, maybe you and Sarah could join us? Let me know if you can come. Hope to see you on Sunday.

Love,

Melanie

Email C

Dear Malcolm,

I'm writing to let you know that I need to rearrange my trip to New York, planned for next week. David Smith, our new managing director, has just asked me to go with him to Beijing on Sunday to attend a meeting with our Chinese distributor. I'm very sorry to cancel my trip at the last minute, but the meeting in China is really important.

Could we hold a meeting in New York the week of May 15 instead? Let me know if you're free to meet that week.

Best,

Amanda

b Read the three emails again. Are the sentences true or false?

1 Mr. Patterson didn't stay in the same hotel as his friends.
2 The agents in Turkey couldn't find a hotel for Mr. Patterson's family.
3 Turkish Sun Tours is going to give Mr. Patterson a free vacation.
4 Melanie would like to invite Jim and Sarah to lunch next Sunday.
5 Amanda wants to meet Malcolm in Beijing next week.

2 WRITING SKILLS
Formal and informal language

a Read the sentences from an email from the manager of a restaurant to an unhappy customer. Rewrite the sentences and change the words in **bold** to make the email more formal.

1 **Hi** Mrs. Miller,
Dear Mrs. Miller,
2 **Thanks** very much for your email of June 15.
3 **I'm** writing to **say sorry** for the poor service you received in our restaurant last Saturday.
4 **We've** just opened the restaurant, and **we've** had a few problems finding experienced servers.
5 However, **we're** working hard to improve our levels of service, and **I'm** confident that we **won't** have any more problems like this in the future.
6 We hope **you'll** come back to our restaurant again, and **we'd** like to offer you a 50% discount on your next meal with us.
7 This is our way of **saying sorry** for the problems **you've** had.
8 **Best wishes,**

3 WRITING

a Read the letter from David Hurst to a hotel in Cartagena. Write an email of apology from the manager of the hotel. Use the notes to help you.

July 10, 2020

Re: Problems at Hotel Dante

Dear Sir/Madam,

I am writing to complain about the poor service I received when I stayed at your hotel in Cartagena last week.

First, when I booked the room online, I asked for a room with an ocean view. However, I was given a room with a view of the parking lot. Second, the receptionist was very rude to my wife when she had a problem with the shower. In fact, there wasn't enough hot water for us to take a shower for the first two days of our stay. Finally, the service in the restaurant was too slow. Every morning we had to wait at least half an hour for our breakfast.

I look forward to hearing from you.

Sincerely,

David Hurst

Notes for reply to Mr. Hurst

- *apologize for poor service*
- *wrong room: problems with website?*
- *shower: problems with water heating system*
- *slow service in restaurant: three servers sick that week*
- *offer a 50% discount on next visit?*

UNIT 10
Reading and listening extension

1 READING

a Read the magazine article. Match the people 1–3 with the phrases a–c.

1 Isabella	a too difficult
2 Eduardo	b concentrate better
3 Caitlin	c more relaxed

(Example: 1 Isabella — b concentrate better)

b Read the article again and check (✓) the correct endings to the sentences.

1 In the magazine article, three people were asked …
- a ☐ what they thought about smartphones and technology.
- b ☑ not to use their smartphone for a week.
- c ☐ to imagine a world without technology.

2 Isabella thought that she would …
- a ☐ not be involved with other people if she didn't have her phone.
- b ☐ break up with her boyfriend if she didn't have her phone.
- c ☐ enjoy not having to use her phone.

3 Isabella realized that …
- a ☐ she didn't have enough time to spend with her friends.
- b ☐ she thought less about what other people were doing when she didn't have her phone.
- c ☐ she wasn't talking to her friends enough.

4 If Eduardo didn't have his phone, …
- a ☐ he thought there would be serious problems with his business.
- b ☐ he thought he would have to work more in the evenings.
- c ☐ he wouldn't be able to make decisions.

5 Caitlin didn't want to stop using her phone because …
- a ☐ she liked using it to read about fashion.
- b ☐ she needed it for her job.
- c ☐ she was worried that people wouldn't call her.

c Read the article again and check (✓) the correct people. Sometimes there is more than one possible answer.

1 Who had a better private life without a smartphone?
a ☑ Isabella b ☑ Eduardo c ☐ Caitlin

2 Who thought they wouldn't be able to take care of something properly without their phone?
a ☐ Isabella b ☐ Eduardo c ☐ Caitlin

3 Who realized that they didn't have to do things immediately?
a ☐ Isabella b ☐ Eduardo c ☐ Caitlin

4 Who was right to be worried about not having a phone?
a ☐ Isabella b ☐ Eduardo c ☐ Caitlin

5 Who realized that their social life would continue without a phone?
a ☐ Isabella b ☐ Eduardo c ☐ Caitlin

6 Who learned something positive from the experiment?
a ☐ Isabella b ☐ Eduardo c ☐ Caitlin

7 Who didn't complete the experiment?
a ☐ Isabella b ☐ Eduardo c ☐ Caitlin

8 Who found that not communicating was a problem for their work?
a ☐ Isabella b ☐ Eduardo c ☐ Caitlin

d Write about what you would do if you couldn't use your phone for a week.

- How would you communicate with friends?
- How would you feel?
- What would the advantages and disadvantages be?

Please Turn Off Your Phones!

In the world today, over 3 billion (3,000,000,000) people own a smartphone, and over 80% of them say that they never turn it off. We use smartphones for everything, from making phone calls to being our personal fitness trainers. With over 5,000,000 apps available, it seems that there isn't too much they can't do.

But imagine if you had to live without your smartphone for a week. What would you do?

We asked three users to try.

ISABELLA, 17, STUDENT, MADRID, SPAIN
If I didn't have my phone for a week, I wouldn't be able to live. It's too important to be without. That's what I thought. When I feel like chatting with my friends, I'll use my phone. I even broke up with my last boyfriend using my phone. Without it, I wouldn't be able to know everything that's happening. But this week, I actually enjoyed not having it. I could concentrate better, I wasn't too worried about what everyone was saying or doing, and I spent more time actually talking to my friends.

EDUARDO, 46, BUSINESSMAN, MEXICO CITY, MEXICO
I'm on my smartphone all day. If I couldn't use it for a week, I wouldn't be able to take care of my business. It would be a disaster. Well, that's what I thought – but it wasn't. I worked more effectively when I was in the office, I had more time to think about everything, and in the evenings, I was a lot more relaxed. I realized that I could put off making decisions until I was in the office. It's really changed how I work, and I think the business is actually doing better now.

CAITLIN, 24, FASHION WRITER, NEW YORK CITY, U.S.
I write a fashion blog. If I couldn't use my phone, I wouldn't have a job. It's what I do and who I am. When I find out something, I need to pass it on, quickly. That's why people read my blog. I tried it for a day, but it was too difficult. I couldn't take any photos of cool people on the streets or quickly add something to my blog when I was out at a party. I just wasn't doing enough. It was horrible.

2 LISTENING

a ▶10.06 Listen to the conversation and underline the people who said these things.

1 Buying something at a store is usually more expensive than buying online.
Zuza / Haluk / No one
2 When you buy online, you can't get what you buy right away.
Zuza / Haluk / No one
3 Buying clothes can be difficult because you cannot try them on before you buy them.
Zuza / Haluk / No one
4 You cannot return something that you buy online.
Zuza / Haluk / No one
5 There are sometimes problems with the delivery of things you buy online.
Zuza / Haluk / No one
6 If people stopped going to stores, they would all close.
Zuza / Haluk / No one

b ▶10.06 Listen to the conversation again and check (✓) the correct endings to the sentences.

1 Haluk thinks online shopping is better because …
 a ☑ you can buy things at any time of the day, and it is often cheaper.
 b ☐ you don't have to leave your house, and it is often cheaper.
 c ☐ you don't have to wait more than a few days, and it is cheaper.
2 The coat that Haluk bought recently was …
 a ☐ damaged in the mail.
 b ☐ too big for him.
 c ☐ the wrong size and color.
3 The company that sold the coat …
 a ☐ has given him an explanation of what happened.
 b ☐ has given him a refund.
 c ☐ hasn't replied to his email.
4 Haluk buys books online because …
 a ☐ he doesn't like going to bookstores.
 b ☐ he can find more books online than in the bookstore.
 c ☐ the bookstore in his town has closed.
5 Zuza thinks that online shopping …
 a ☐ will have an effect on stores in the future.
 b ☐ has already had an effect on stores in her town.
 c ☐ is more fun than normal shopping.
6 Which of the statements is not true?
 a ☐ Zuza hopes that she will meet someone when she is shopping.
 b ☐ Zuza thinks that Haluk should stop buying things online.
 c ☐ Zuza thinks that Haluk will meet someone while he is at home.

c Write about the advantages and disadvantages of shopping online. Include answers to these questions:

- What have you bought online?
- Why did you buy it online?
- Did you have any problems buying it online?

Review and extension

1 GRAMMAR

Correct the sentences.

1 This table isn't enough big for 20 people.
This table isn't big enough for 20 people.
2 He invited too much people to his party – over 100!
3 If I would have a motorcycle, I wouldn't take the bus to work.
4 This morning it was too cold for swim in the ocean.
5 I will go on a diet if I were overweight.
6 If Chile would win the World Cup, he would be delighted.

2 VOCABULARY

Correct the sentences.

1 Could you care of my cat while I'm on vacation?
Could you take care of my cat while I'm on vacation?
2 Tim isn't here right now, but I can pass a message.
3 There's a very small menu in that restaurant, so the choose of food is very limited.
4 It's sad that Anna and Esteban have broken down after being together for ten years.
5 If you're not happy with your hotel, you should complaint.
6 She was offered a better job, but she turned it off.

3 WORDPOWER
Multi-word verbs with *on*

Underline the correct words to complete the sentences.

1 He *got / tried / kept* on the shoes, but they were too big.
2 I can't *go / put / get* on working so much – I'm exhausted!
3 It was pretty dark in the restaurant, so I had to *get / carry / put* on my glasses to read the menu.
4 I'm not sleeping well because my neighbor's dog *puts / keeps / tries* on barking all night long.
5 It was a really cold day, so she decided to *put / try / carry* on her scarf and gloves.
6 Although it started raining, we decided to *put / try / keep* on playing tennis for another 20 minutes.
7 He stopped playing video games and *tried / got / put* on with his homework.
8 Although they were dirty, I *kept / put / went* my shoes on when I went into his house.

REVIEW YOUR PROGRESS

Look again at Review Your Progress on p. 106 of the Student's Book. How well can you do these things now?
3 = very well 2 = well 1 = not so well

I CAN …	
talk about moral dilemmas	☐
describe problems with goods and services	☐
return goods and make complaints	☐
write an apology email.	☐

11A IT'S A ROBOT THAT LOOKS LIKE A HUMAN

1 GRAMMAR Defining relative clauses

a Complete the sentences with *who, which,* or *where.*

1 Charles Dickens was the English author __who__ wrote *Oliver Twist.*
2 The Louvre is the museum in Paris ________ you can see the famous *Mona Lisa* by Leonardo da Vinci.
3 Last night we watched a TV show ________ explained the causes of World War I.
4 When I was on vacation, I met a man ________ worked for CNN in Atlanta.
5 This is the place in New Zealand ________ they made the movie *The Lord of the Rings.*
6 Tim Berners-Lee was the scientist ________ invented the World Wide Web in the early 1990s.
7 That's the app ________ counts your steps every day.
8 Near where I work, there's a gym ________ only costs $20 per month.
9 He knows a restaurant near the train station ________ you can have a delicious three-course meal for only $10.
10 Maria's got an aunt in England ________ has been married four times!

b Correct the sentences.

1 There are some beautiful boots in that store who cost only $35!
There are some beautiful boots in that store which cost only $35!
OR
There are some beautiful boots in that store that cost only $35!
2 There's a woman over there which used to work for your company.
____
3 There's a café near me it has 50 different kinds of tea!
____
4 My dad has a cousin in Houston he works for NASA.
____
5 I know an Italian restaurant in London that you can have chocolate spaghetti!
____
6 I have a new phone who also comes with free music apps.
____
7 That's a movie theater where they're showing the new Superman movie next week.
____
8 He just bought a new TV it has amazing picture quality.
____

2 VOCABULARY Compound nouns

a Complete the crossword puzzle.

→ Across
3 I bought my boots at the new s*hoe* s*tore* across from the café.
4 *Blade Runner* is a s______ f______ story.
5 Why don't we meet in front of the movie t______?
8 Can you read that r______ s______ on the side of the highway?
11 Billy Joe from the band Green Day is one of her favorite r______ s______.

↓ Down
1 The first time the TV s______ *Star Trek* was shown was in 1966.
2 Can you get me six c______ cups from the cupboard, please?
4 The movie *Forrest Gump* was also famous for its s______. It had so many great songs.
6 I'm sure I wrote down her telephone number in my a______ book.
7 The street l______ turn on automatically when it starts getting dark.
9 At the end of the day, her eyes are tired from looking at the computer s______.
10 Can you imagine a future with driverless c______? What will people do while they're on the highway?

3 PRONUNCIATION Word stress: compound nouns

a 11.01 Listen to the compound nouns and underline the main stressed syllable.

1 mountain climbing
2 computer screen
3 science fiction
4 address book
5 bread knife
6 parking lot
7 coffee cup
8 bookshelf

11B I THINK THEY DISCOVERED IT BY CHANCE

1 GRAMMAR Articles

a Complete the conversation at a tourist office with the correct articles: *a*, *an*, *the*, or Ø.

A Good morning. Please take [1] *a* seat. I'll be with you in [2]______ moment ... Now, how can I help you?
B Could you help us find [3]______ hotel in [4]______ Miami, please?
A Yes, of course. Would you like [5]______ hotel in South Beach?
B Yes, if possible.
A OK, how about [6]______ Paradise Hotel? They have some available rooms.
B Do they have [7]______ free parking?
A Yes, they do, but you can walk to all the great places! It's about a five-minute walk to [8]______ Ocean Drive. And it's across the street from [9]______ beach. It's one of [10]______ nicest hotels in all of Miami.
B Great. Can you ask if they have [11]______ double room for three nights? And can you check [12]______ price?
A Yes, sure. I'm afraid [13]______ hotels in Miami are really expensive. A lot of [14]______ people think that Miami's [15]______ most expensive beach city for [16]______ tourists in [17]______ U.S.
B Yes, [18]______ hotel that we stayed in last year cost over $300 a night!
A OK, I've booked it for you. If you're coming from [19]______ highway, go down [20]______ Alton Road and make a left on 7th Street. It's on [21]______ left, across from [22]______ beach.
B Great. Thank you very much.

b 11.02 Listen and check.

c Correct the sentences.

1 That movie was most exciting thriller I've ever seen.
That movie was the most exciting thriller I've ever seen.
2 In the U.K., the police officers don't usually carry guns.
______
3 I love the Italian ice cream. It's the best in the world!
______
4 They drove to Paris by car and then stayed in the beautiful hotel near the Eiffel Tower.
______
5 France is the most popular country for the tourists in the world.
______
6 Doctors in U.S. are paid much more than nurses.
______

2 VOCABULARY Adverbials: luck and chance

a Match 1–8 with a–h to make sentences.

1 [f] I didn't have enough money to pay the taxi driver, but fortunately,
2 [ ] He didn't train very hard for his first marathon, but amazingly,
3 [ ] I didn't break your phone on purpose. I
4 [ ] While they were moving the furniture around, they accidentally
5 [ ] The president was very popular so, as expected,
6 [ ] We got to the airport on time, but unfortunately,
7 [ ] My grandma fell again yesterday, but luckily,
8 [ ] I found these old letters from my uncle by chance

a accidentally dropped it while I was getting out of the car.
b he won the election very easily with 75% of the vote.
c while I was fixing the old desk in my aunt's bedroom.
d broke my computer screen.
e our flight to Costa Rica was delayed because of the storms.
f my friend had five dollars that she lent me.
g he finished it in just under three hours.
h she didn't break her arm this time.

b Underline the correct words to complete the sentences.

1 *Surprisingly* / *As expected*, Real Madrid beat the third division team very easily, winning 6 – 0.
2 *Luckily* / *Unfortunately*, I lost my front door key, so I can't get into my house.
3 The ruins of the ancient city were discovered completely *by chance* / *on purpose* while the construction company was building the new highway.
4 *Accidentally* / *Luckily*, it stopped raining in the afternoon, so we were able to take the children to the beach.
5 Sorry, but it was an accident. I didn't do it *on purpose* / *as expected*.
6 *Unfortunately* / *Amazingly*, although he didn't work very hard, he got 95% on his final exam!

3 PRONUNCIATION Word stress: adverbials

a 11.03 Listen to the words and check (✓) the stressed syllable in each word.

1 accidentally
a [ ] ac b [✓] den
2 on purpose
a [ ] pur b [ ] pose
3 by chance
a [ ] by b [ ] chance
4 unfortunately
a [ ] un b [ ] for
5 luckily
a [ ] luc b [ ] ly
6 surprisingly
a [ ] sur b [ ] pri
7 amazingly
a [ ] ma b [ ] zing
8 fortunately
a [ ] for b [ ] nate
9 as expected
a [ ] ex b [ ] pec

11C EVERYDAY ENGLISH
It's straight ahead

1 USEFUL LANGUAGE
Asking for and giving directions in a building

a ▶ 11.04 Listen and put the directions in the correct order.

Can you tell me where the Lincoln Meeting Room is?
☐ Then go up the stairs to the second floor.
☐ The Lincoln Room is the fourth door on the right.
[1] Yes, sure. It's on the second floor.
☐ Then go down to the end of the corridor.
☐ At the top of the stairs, turn left and go down another corridor.
☐ Go through that door over there.
Great, thanks.

b ▶ 11.04 Listen again and check.

c Put the words in the correct order to make sentences.

1 the stairs / first floor / the / to / go down .
Go down the stairs to the first floor.

2 go through / those / and then / doors / down / the corridor .
____

3 down / so, first / to the / go / stairs / the corridor ?
____

4 tell / where / the / you / is, please / staff lounge / me / could ?
____

5 the right / the / down / and it's / the first / on / office / then go / corridor, .
____

6 floor / go / the / to / stairs / the third / up .
____

7 can / check / so, / just / I ?
____

8 I / OK, / think / it / I / got .
____

9 corridor / the top of / the / go / another / right and / stairs, / turn / down / at .
____

10 the meeting room / is / second / left / on / the / door / the .
____

d ▶ 11.05 Listen and check.

2 PRONUNCIATION
Sound and spelling: /ɜr/ and /eər/

a ▶ 11.06 Listen to the words. Check (✓) the sound you hear.

	/ɜr/	/eər/
1 b**ir**d	✓	☐
2 f**ur**	☐	☐
3 **air**	☐	☐
4 wh**ere**	☐	☐
5 w**or**st	☐	☐
6 b**ear**	☐	☐
7 s**ir**	☐	☐
8 f**air**	☐	☐

11D SKILLS FOR WRITING
In my opinion, it's because of the Internet

1 READING

a Read the posts and check (✓) the correct answer.

- a ☐ Bicycles have always been very cheap to buy.
- b ☐ Cycling is a popular hobby for a lot of people.
- c ☐ Cycling is bad for the environment.
- d ☐ Streets with electric lighting were more dangerous.

b Read the posts again. Are the sentences true or false?

1. It was cheaper to have a bicycle than to travel on public transportation.
2. Bicycles are not very popular in the developing world.
3. When a lot of people ride their bikes to work, cities become less polluted.
4. Gas lighting was invented after electric lighting.
5. Reading and writing at night were easier with electric lighting.

The bicycle was invented in the 19th century. At first, bicycles were very expensive, but at the beginning of the 20th century, they were mass-produced in large factories. As a result of this, they became much cheaper, and after that, most people could afford to buy one. Bicycles changed the way people traveled short distances. Because of the bicycle, people who didn't have much money didn't have to travel to work on buses or trains. As a result, they saved money and could get a job farther away from where they lived. Today, bicycles are the most important form of transportation for people in many countries in the developing world. Cycling is also a very popular sport for many people, since it is a great way to stay fit and healthy. In big cities, a lot of people ride their bikes to work, and this helps reduce pollution and protect the environment. Because of this, it seems to me that the bicycle is one of the most important inventions of the last 200 years.

Martin Roberts

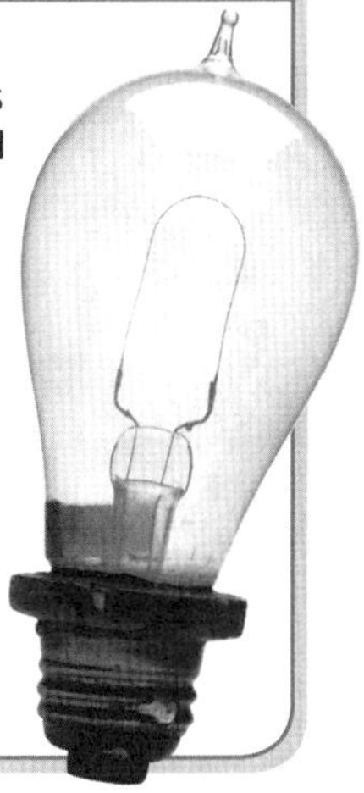

In my opinion, the most important invention is the electric light bulb. The electric light bulb was invented in the 19th century and slowly replaced gas lighting in the streets of big cities and in people's homes. With electric lights, the streets of big cities became safer and, as a result, there was less crime. Also, electric light bulbs improved the lighting in people's houses. As a result, they could do more things when it got dark in the evenings, such as reading books or writing letters. Electric lights have greatly improved the quality of people's lives, and it is hard to imagine life without them.

Naomi Stevens

2 WRITING SKILLS
Expressing results and reasons

a Underline the correct words to complete the sentences.

1. *As a result of* / *Since* / *Because* better windows, new houses lose less heat in winter, and people spend less money on keeping them warm.
2. In the 1960s, people couldn't afford to go to Europe on vacation *because of* / *since* / *as a result of* air travel was so expensive.
3. People didn't use their cell phones when they were traveling abroad *as a result of* / *because of* / *because* phone calls were so expensive.
4. Computers are much smaller now *since* / *because* / *because of* the invention of the microchip.
5. *Since* / *As a result of* / *Because of* you can now travel by train from London to Paris in less than three hours, I won't need to fly anymore.
6. Nowadays, malaria is less common in Africa *since* / *as a result of* / *because* the new vaccination program.
7. *Because* / *Since* / *Because of* the terrible pollution, many European cities only allow people to drive their cars on certain days of the month.
8. She decided to buy a tablet *because of* / *because* / *as a result of* it was much easier to carry around than her old laptop.

3 WRITING

a Write a post about the invention of cell phones. Use the notes to help you.

Notes for post about cell phones

- most important invention = cell phone
- before: had to be home, office, or public phone booth
- keep in contact with friends, family, coworkers
- speak wherever you are: street, supermarket, car, train
- stay in touch with children + elderly relatives
- useful if accident or to call the police
- not only calls and texts: also photos, videos, music, Internet, Facebook
- my phone = my most useful possession: where would I be without it?

Reading and listening extension

1 READING

a Read the story and complete the sentences.

1 Juliane and her _mother_ took a flight from Lima to Pucallpa.
2 The ____________ was hit by lightning.
3 The plane crashed in the ____________.
4 Juliane found some ____________ to eat.
5 Juliane followed a small ____________ through the forest.
6 Some men found Juliane and took her down the river in a ____________.
7 A small airplane flew her to the ____________ in Pucallpa.

b Read the story again. Are the sentences true or false?

1 Juliane was the only person who did not die in the crash.
2 The food that she found belonged to the other passengers.
3 Juliane was not prepared for life in the rainforest.
4 There were people in the hut that Juliane found.
5 The men who found Juliane had a small airplane.

c Read the story again. Match 1–6 with a–f to make sentences.

1 The flight which
2 The bone that
3 The lessons that
4 The boat which
5 The men who
6 The hospital where

a found Juliane took her down the river.
b Juliane broke was in her neck.
c Juliane found belonged to the men who helped her.
d Juliane was on crashed in the rainforest.
e Juliane's father taught her helped her survive.
f Juliane was taken was in Pucallpa.

d Imagine you are Juliane. Write a letter to a friend explaining your experience in the forest. Remember to include:

- what happened to you
- how you felt at the time
- how you feel now.

Amazing but True

There are many true stories about people who have been in a plane crash but didn't die, but what happened to Juliane Koepcke is one of the most amazing stories.

Juliane and her parents lived in Peru. On December 24 in 1971, 17-year-old Juliane was on a plane that was flying from Lima to Pucallpa in Peru with her mother, Maria. They were traveling to meet Juliane's father, who was working in Pucallpa.

Unfortunately, the plane never arrived. During the flight, it was hit by lightning and broke up above the rainforest. Juliane fell over 3,000 meters to the ground and landed still in her seat, and amazingly, still alive. Everyone else on board died. Juliane had a broken bone in her neck and cuts on her arms, but surprisingly, she could still walk.

First of all, she tried to find her mother. Unfortunately, she couldn't see her, so she decided to look for some food instead. Luckily, she found some candy that passengers had taken with them for the Christmas holiday. This was the only food that she found to eat.

Juliane's father was a biologist who had spent a lot of time in the rainforests in Peru with his family. Fortunately, he had taught Juliane some important lessons in how to stay alive. The skills that Juliane had learned helped her in the rainforest. When she found a small river, she knew that if she followed it, it would take her to a town. It also gave her fresh water to drink and a natural path through the forest.

She walked and swam for nine days until, as expected, she found an empty hut made of wood. By chance, she also found a boat. Juliane wanted to leave, but she didn't want to take the boat because it wasn't hers. So she waited. Luckily, hours later the men who used the hut came back and found Juliane. They helped take care of her. The next day, they took her in the boat down the river to a place where there was a small airplane, which could take her to the hospital in Pucallpa. No one really knows why Juliane lived and everyone else died on the flight, but everyone agrees that it is an amazing story.

2 LISTENING

a 11.07 Listen to the conversation. Number the events in the correct order.

- ☐ The police arrived.
- ☐ The car with one man inside drove into the cash machine.
- ☐ The men drove the car into something in the street.
- ☐ The men ran away into a park.
- ☐ The men took some money from the cash machine.
- ☐ The men tried to break open the cash machine.
- [1] A car with two men inside drove into the cash machine very fast.

b 11.07 Listen to the conversation again and check (✓) the correct answers.

1 Where was Monica Edwards when the vehicle crashed into the cash machine?
  a ☐ in the bedroom
  b ☐ in the bathroom
  c ☑ in another room

2 At first, Monica thought the crash was …
  a ☐ an accident.
  b ☐ amazing.
  c ☐ done on purpose.

3 What did the men use to try and break open the machine?
  a ☐ something they found in the street
  b ☐ something they were wearing
  c ☐ something that was in the car

4 One of the men …
  a ☐ was wearing dark glasses.
  b ☐ looked like a baseball player.
  c ☐ was much older than the other man.

5 What happened when they opened the cash machine?
  a ☐ They were able to take a lot of money.
  b ☐ The police came.
  c ☐ The men decided to run away.

6 Why didn't the men drive away?
  a ☐ They didn't have the key to the car.
  b ☐ The car was damaged.
  c ☐ The police stopped them.

c Write about a surprising or amazing thing you may have seen. Remember to include:

- what you saw
- what happened
- how you felt.

Review and extension

1 GRAMMAR

Correct the sentences.

1 *Rocky* was the movie what Sylvester Stallone made in 1976.
  Rocky was the movie that Sylvester Stallone made in 1976.
2 Sorry, I can't talk to you right now because I'm at the work.
3 Generally speaking, most the men like watching sports on TV.
4 Modern Living is the store who I bought my leather sofa.
5 Look! That's a man who stole my wallet!
6 John F. Kennedy was the American president which was assassinated in Dallas in 1963.

2 VOCABULARY

Correct the sentences.

1 They're having a sale at the shoe store next to the theater movie.
  They're having a sale at the shoe store next to the movie theater.
2 I think I wrote his phone number in my book address.
3 Surprisedly, it tasted a little like chicken.
4 I'm afraid of heights, so I don't want to go rockclimbing.
5 He opened the car's door without looking and hit an old man on a bicycle.
6 I'm sorry I broke your cup of coffee – it was an accident.

3 WORDPOWER Preposition + noun

Match 1–6 with a–f to make sentences.

1 [f] Their plane didn't leave on
2 ☐ My parents are still in
3 ☐ I didn't break your glasses on
4 ☐ All of the bank robbers are now in
5 ☐ There are a lot of computers for
6 ☐ Next time you come to town, tell me in

a love with each other after 30 years of marriage.
b sale on eBay. I might get one.
c advance so I can book some theater tickets.
d prison, aside from the one who escaped.
e purpose. I sat on them by mistake.
f time. It was 30 minutes late.

REVIEW YOUR PROGRESS

Look again at Review Your Progress on p. 116 of the Student's Book. How well can you do these things now?
3 = very well 2 = well 1 = not so well

I CAN …	
explain what technology does	☐
talk about discoveries	☐
ask for and give directions in a building	☐
write a post expressing an opinion.	☐

12A I HAD ALWAYS THOUGHT THEY WERE DANGEROUS

1 VOCABULARY Animals

a Complete the crossword puzzle.

→ Across

3 This insect bites humans and drinks their blood. mosquito
5 This animal lives in deserts and can travel long distances without food or water. ________
6 This insect produces honey. ________
7 This bird is large, very colorful, and can learn to "talk" by copying what someone says to it. ________

↓ Down

1 This animal has eight legs and makes webs to catch small flies. One of the biggest kinds is the tarantula. ________
2 This animal is the largest kind of monkey in the world. ________
4 The blue ________ is the biggest animal on the planet.
8 This is the largest animal of the cat family and is orange with black stripes. ________

2 GRAMMAR Past perfect

a Complete the sentences with the past perfect forms of the verbs in the box.

steal work get up miss stop ~~leave~~ begin finish

1 By the time we got to the station, my sister's train had already left.
2 When my grandmother called, I ________ just ________ doing my homework.
3 He ________ really hard at school all year, so he got excellent grades on his exams.
4 Anthony arrived late for school this morning because he ________ late.
5 When they got to the movie theater, the movie ________ just ________.
6 When he got back from vacation, he found that someone ________ his car.
7 We had to take a taxi home from the train station because we ________ the last bus.
8 The two men ________ arguing by the time the police arrived.

b Complete the text with the simple past or past perfect forms of the verbs in parentheses.

We [1] had (have) a terrible time on our way from London to Barcelona. The problems [2]________ (begin) when we [3]________ (leave) the hotel at 6:30 in the morning. There [4]________ (be) a huge traffic jam on the highway because two trucks [5]________ (crash) and the road [6]________ (be) completely blocked.

By the time we [7]________ (reach) the airport, we [8]________ (miss) our flight. It [9]________ (take) off five minutes before we [10]________ (arrive) at the check-in counter. We [11]________ (try) to buy some tickets for the next flight to Barcelona, but they [12]________ (sell) out. In the end, we [13]________ (buy) tickets for a flight at 7 p.m. and [14]________ (spend) the whole day at the airport.

We [15]________ (land) in Barcelona at 9:45, but we [16]________ (not collect) our suitcases from baggage claim until 11 o'clock because there [17]________ (be) a baggage handlers' strike that day. By the time our taxi driver [18]________ (find) our hotel, the restaurant [19]________ (close), so we [20]________ (go) straight to bed without having dinner.

3 PRONUNCIATION Sound and spelling: /ʌ/, /ɔ/, and /oʊ/

a 12.01 Look at the words and listen to the pronunciation of the letters in **bold**. Complete the chart with the words in the box.

~~br**ou**ght~~ c**o**me d**o**ne t**a**lked kn**ow**n
sp**o**ken r**u**n t**au**ght w**o**ken w**o**n

/ʌ/ (e.g., dr**u**nk)	/ɔ/ (e.g., b**ou**ght)	/oʊ/ (e.g., ch**o**sen)
	brought	

12B HE SAID I WAS SELFISH!

1 GRAMMAR Reported speech

a Underline the correct words to complete the sentences.

1 Matthew said, "I want to play soccer with my friends."
He *told me* / *said me* / *told* that *we want* / *I wanted* / *he wanted* to play soccer with *my* / *his* / *your* friends.

2 Naomi said, "I'll help you wash the dishes."
She *told* / *said* / *said me* that *she will* / *I would* / *she would* help *me* / *her* / *you* wash the dishes.

3 Angela said, "My mom's watching a movie with my little brother."
She *told* / *told me* / *said me* that *my* / *his* / *her* mom *had watched* / *was watching* / *watching* a movie with *her* / *his* / *my* little brother.

4 David said, "We went to the park with some friends from our school."
He *said* / *told* / *said me* that *they've gone* / *they'd gone* / *we've gone* to the park with some friends from *our* / *her* / *their* school.

5 James said, "Andy, my dad can't take us to the zoo on Saturday."
He *said me* / *told him* / *said him* that *my* / *her* / *his* dad *couldn't* / *could* / *didn't can* take *us* / *them* / *me* to the zoo on Saturday.

6 Josh said, "I think that we'll go to the beach with our cousins after lunch."
He *told* / *told us* / *said us* that he *is thinking* / *thought* / *had thought* that *we will go* / *he would go* / *they would go* to the beach with *my* / *their* / *her* cousins after lunch.

7 She said, "I've already done all of my homework."
She *said* / *told* / *said me* that *she already did* / *I've already done* / *she'd already done* all of *my* / *his* / *her* homework.

8 Adam said, "My little sister isn't going to come to my birthday party!"
He *told* / *told us* / *said us* that *my* / *her* / *his* little sister *isn't going to* / *wasn't going to* / *not going to* come to *his* / *her* / *our* birthday party.

b Read the direct speech sentences. Use reported speech to report what the speaker said. Make any necessary changes to the highlighted words.

1 "I'm waiting for my bus to come."
She said she was waiting for her bus to come. OR She said that she was waiting for her bus to come.

2 "I'll invite you and your brother to my house for dinner next week."
He told me …

3 "You can use my computer to do your homework."
She told James …

4 "The traffic was really bad, so we missed the 5:15 train."
He said …

5 "We're going to buy you a wonderful present for your birthday."
She told me …

6 "I've tried calling my friend, but she didn't answer, so I think she's away on vacation."
He said …

2 VOCABULARY Personality adjectives

a Complete the crossword puzzle.

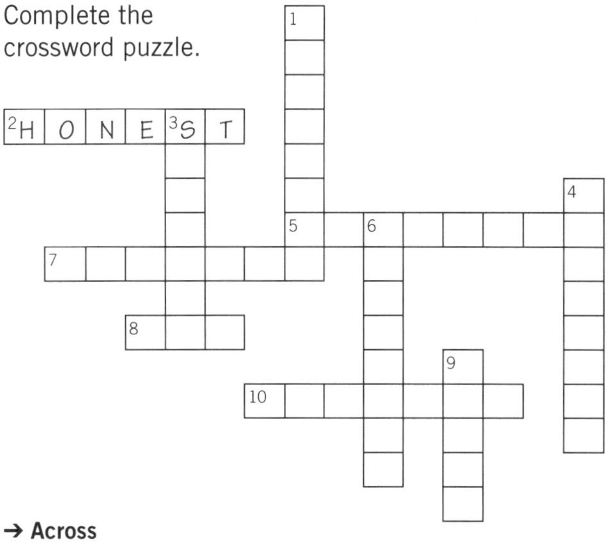

→ **Across**

2 He's so honest! When a sales assistant gave him too much change yesterday, he didn't keep it – he told her she'd made a mistake.

5 She's extremely ________ – she has a lot of friends, and she loves meeting new people.

7 You know, I've never seen Jim laugh, and he rarely smiles – he's always so ________.

8 She's really ________ – she hates having to talk to people she doesn't know at parties.

10 He's a very ________ person – he worries about everything.

↓ **Down**

1 You're so ________! That's the second time you've lost your keys this month.

3 You're so ________ – why should we always do what you want to do? Why can't you think about other people for a change?

4 She's a very ________ person. Although she doesn't have much money, she bought all her friends dinner when it was her birthday.

6 He's a very ________ person – he writes poems and short stories and loves painting.

9 Mike's a really ________ guy – he's always telling us jokes and making us laugh.

12C EVERYDAY ENGLISH
I think that's the quickest way

1 USEFUL LANGUAGE Agreeing and disagreeing

a Match 1–8 with a–h to make exchanges.

1 [g] I believe yoga is a great way to relax before you go to bed.
2 [ ] I think Brazil has the best soccer team in the world.
3 [ ] In my opinion, Venice is a more attractive city than Florence.
4 [ ] This is a nicer movie theater than the one we went to last week.
5 [ ] Barcelona is the biggest city in Spain.
6 [ ] Leonardo DiCaprio is a better actor than Brad Pitt.
7 [ ] In my opinion, Italian coffee is better than French coffee.
8 [ ] I think the weather in the U.K. in winter is much better than in Germany.

a I don't think so. I think there are more people in Madrid, actually.
b That's true. He was amazing in *The Revenant.*
c I agree. The seats are very comfortable, and the screen is wider.
d I'm not sure about that. I think Argentina will beat them in the final.
e That could be. It's such a beautiful place to visit. I love it!
f I'm afraid I don't agree. It rains so much there in January and February. I can't stand it!
g You're absolutely right. I try and do a few exercises every night.
h I'm sorry, but how do you know? You don't drink coffee!

b 12.02 Listen and check.

c Underline the correct words to complete the exchanges.

1 **A** I think the Amazon is the longest river in the world.
B *That could be. / <u>I don't think so</u>. / That's true.* Actually, I think the Nile is longer than the Amazon.
2 **A** Swiss chocolate is much better than British chocolate.
B *You're absolutely right. / Oh, please. / I'm not sure about that.* It's probably the best in the world.
3 **A** Russian is a harder language to learn than Spanish.
B *Oh, please. / I don't think so. / That could be.* In my opinion, Spanish is one of the easiest languages to learn.
4 **A** Everybody should retire when they reach 60.
B *That's right. / Oh, please. / Exactly.* That's way too early! Older people have so much experience that they can pass on to their younger coworkers.
5 **A** Tablets are so much more practical than laptops.
B *I'm sorry, but I don't agree. / I'm afraid you're wrong. / That's true.* They're much lighter and easier to carry.
6 **A** His last movie was amazing!
B *I'm not sure about that. / You're right. / I don't think so.* It's the best movie he's made so far.

d 12.03 Listen and check.

2 PRONUNCIATION Main stress: contrastive

a 12.04 Listen to the exchanges and check (✓) the stressed word in each of B's responses.

	Stressed word
1 **A** Antonio Banderas is a Mexican actor. **B** Um, he's actually a Spanish actor.	Spanish ✓ actor
2 **A** French food's the best in the world. **B** Well, actually, I think Italian food is the best.	Italian food
3 **A** I like the American English accent. **B** Do you? I prefer British English, actually.	British English
4 **A** New York's the best place to live in the U.S. **B** Actually, I think San Francisco's the best place.	San Francisco best
5 **A** I think Chelsea will win the Champions League this year. **B** No way! Barcelona will win it this year.	Barcelona win
6 **A** Baseball is the most popular sport in Mexico. **B** I'm sorry, but I think soccer is the most popular sport.	soccer sport

12D SKILLS FOR WRITING

A few hours later, they started baking again

1 READING

a Read the text and check (✓) the correct answer.

a ☐ The old woman lost her bag in the park.
b ☐ The thief gave the bag back to the old woman.
c ☐ The police officers thought Tom had stolen a bag.
d ☐ Tom stopped a man who had taken a woman's bag.

b Read the text again. Are the sentences true or false?

1 Tom was walking across the park with Brian when he heard the old woman.
2 The young man couldn't escape because Tom was sitting on him.
3 Both police officers asked Tom to explain what had happened.
4 Tom didn't want to accept the old woman's money at first.
5 The old woman didn't have much money.

2 WRITING SKILLS
Linkers: past time

a Underline the correct words to complete the sentences.

1 *As soon as* / *After a while* the police arrived, the man started running down the street.
2 He saw the strange man with the black dog at 7:30 in the morning. *By morning* / *Later that day*, he saw him again, but this time without his dog.
3 They said goodnight and went back to their hotel to sleep. *As soon as* / *The next morning*, they caught the train to Paris.
4 It started to snow late last night. *By morning*, / *After a while*, when we woke up, the entire city was covered in snow!
5 The sky was covered in dark clouds. *A few hours later* / *Later that year*, it started to rain very heavily.

Local Hero

One hot day last July, Tom was walking home from college after playing a baseball game. He had just said goodbye to his best friend, Brian, and was walking through the park near his house when he heard someone shouting, "Stop, thief!" He turned around and saw an old woman. She was pointing at a young man in his early twenties who was running toward him. "He stole my bag!" she shouted. The thief was coming toward Tom, and the old woman shouted at him, "Hey, you! Stop him!" A few seconds later, Tom threw himself at the young man, and the thief fell down on the path. Tom immediately sat on the thief's back so he couldn't escape. A few minutes later, Tom heard a siren and saw the flashing lights of a police car. The old woman had called the police on her cell phone and, luckily, a police car had been near the park at the time.

Two police officers got out of the car quickly and ran toward Tom and the thief as fast as they could. As soon as they got to Tom, they immediately arrested the young man. While one of them took him to the police car, the other started asking Tom and the old woman some questions about what had happened. Tom gave the old woman her bag. Fortunately, everything was still inside it. The old woman thanked Tom and asked him for his telephone number. She explained that she had to leave because she was going to visit a friend in the hospital. When the old woman had gone, Tom told the police officer what had happened, and he wrote everything down in his notebook. Finally, he gave the police officer his phone number and went home.

The next day, the old woman called Tom. She thanked him again and invited him to her house. She said that she wanted to give him a reward. Later that week, Tom went to visit the old woman at her house. She lived in a big house near the park, and there was a Rolls-Royce in front of it. While they talked, she made him some coffee and gave him some delicious chocolate cake. Then, just as he was standing up to leave, she opened her bag and gave him $500. Tom told her that he didn't want to take it, but she insisted: "Please take it. I have plenty of money, and I'd really like to thank you for being so brave." In the end, Tom agreed to take it. By the end of the week, he had used the money to buy a new laptop.

3 WRITING

a David went on a hiking trip in Utah last year. Write a story about what happened. Use the time expressions in the box and the notes to help you.

about an hour later · a few minutes later · after a while · later that day · as soon as · the next day · by the next day · soon · last year · when

Notes on accident during hiking trip

- Utah + 3 friends
- accident – top of a mountain? eating sandwiches?
- weather changed – heavy snow – only see 20 meters
- started hiking down path: next town (spend the night?)
- snow: getting deeper?
- all confident hikers: no problems?
- shout from behind me: Anthony lying on the ground (fallen over a rock?)
- leg hurting badly: broken?
- call for help? Cell phone: emergency services
- mountain rescue team (helicopter)
- arrived hospital
- leg not badly broken: no need to operate and he could leave the hospital the next day – all felt very relieved

UNIT 12

Reading and listening extension

We Bought a Zoo

In March 2005, Benjamin Mee received a letter from his sister. Inside was an ad for a house that was for sale. It was a house with a zoo full of animals in its backyard.

Earlier that year, Benjamin's father had died, and his mother was living alone in a large house in London, which she was trying to sell for $1.5 million, the same price as the zoo. Benjamin, who was living in France with his wife and two children, thought that it would be wonderful for his family to sell his mother's house and buy the zoo so that they could all live together and take care of each other. He knew that his father, a sensible man, would not have agreed. But Benjamin was thinking of the future.

Surprisingly, his family agreed. Benjamin's mother was very generous and happy to buy the zoo after selling her house. The year before, she had spent a day at a zoo helping the zookeepers and had really enjoyed taking care of the animals. Benjamin's wife was more anxious. She was very sick and didn't want to change her life, but Benjamin said that it would help her and the children think about something else.

Unfortunately, buying the zoo was pretty difficult, but Benjamin was patient and confident, and after a year of trying, in October 2006, they did it. But four days after the family moved into the zoo, there was a disaster. A jaguar, a large spotted cat, had escaped after a zookeeper had forgotten to close a door. The family also needed over $600,000 for repairs before they could open the zoo. Then while they were doing the repairs, Benjamin's wife died.

On July 7, 2007, the zoo opened, and the first visitors came to see the animals. There were tigers, bears, monkeys, parrots, snakes, and spiders, and a lot of other animals. People loved the zoo and loved what Benjamin, his children, who were always sociable and friendly with visitors, and his family had done.

In 2008, he wrote a book called *We Bought a Zoo*, which became very popular. A Hollywood producer read the story and decided to make a movie about it. In 2012, the movie was released, and the money Benjamin earned from it helped pay the bills and keep the zoo open.

If you'd like to visit the zoo that Benjamin's family bought, it's called the Dartmoor Zoological Gardens, in southwest England.

1 READING

a Read the magazine article above. Put the events in the correct order.

- [ ] Benjamin and his family buy the zoo.
- [1] Benjamin's mother spends a day at a zoo.
- [ ] The zoo opens.
- [ ] Benjamin's father dies.
- [ ] A Hollywood movie is made about the zoo.
- [ ] Benjamin receives a letter from his sister.

b Read the magazine article again. Match the adjectives and the descriptions with the people. Complete the chart with the words in the boxes.

Adjectives	Descriptions
anxious	friendly with people
generous	gave a lot of money to buy something
~~patient~~	~~waited a year to do something~~
sociable	was worried about changing something

	Adjective	Description
1 Benjamin	*patient*	*waited a year to do something*
2 Benjamin's wife		
3 Benjamin's mother		
4 Benjamin's children		

c Read the magazine article again. Check (✓) the correct responses.

1 Why did Benjamin want to buy the zoo?
   a [ ] He had always wanted to work with animals.
   b [✓] He wanted to bring his family closer at a difficult time.
   c [ ] His mother was a zookeeper.

2 How did the jaguar escape?
   a [ ] The zookeeper hadn't done something that was important.
   b [ ] The zoo needed to be repaired.
   c [ ] A visitor opened the door.

3 Benjamin's wife died …
   a [ ] before Benjamin bought the zoo.
   b [ ] before the zoo opened.
   c [ ] when the zoo opened.

4 How did the Hollywood movie help Benjamin and the zoo?
   a [ ] A lot of people visited the zoo after they saw the movie.
   b [ ] Benjamin wrote a book about it.
   c [ ] The money he got helped run the zoo.

d Write a paragraph about a trip that you have recently been on. Remember to include:

- where you went
- what you did
- what you had to prepare before you went
- what you thought of the trip.

2 LISTENING

a 12.05 Listen to the conversation. Put the events in the correct order.

- [ ] Brad goes back to the factory to pick up the jewelry.
- [ ] Brad leaves the hostel with 10 dollars.
- [1] Brad meets two brothers in a tea house.
- [ ] Brad runs away and gets in a taxi.
- [ ] The brothers make Brad 30 necklaces.
- [ ] The brothers take Brad to a cash machine.
- [ ] The three men go sightseeing together.
- [ ] The two brothers take Brad to their jewelry factory.

b 12.05 Listen to the conversation again, and read the sentences in direct speech. They are from Brad's story, but he uses reported speech. Check (✓) the correct answers.

1 "We can take you to see some tigers tomorrow."
Who said this?
a [ ] Brad b [ ] Jay c [✓] Viki

2 "I'll buy a small piece."
Who said this?
a [ ] Brad b [ ] Jay c [ ] Viki

3 "It will be ready tomorrow."
What will be ready tomorrow?
a [ ] the money
b [ ] the jewelry
c [ ] the hostel

4 "This is what you asked for yesterday."
What is *this*?
a [ ] a small piece of jewelry
b [ ] 30 necklaces
c [ ] the money

5 "You will have to pay 100 dollars."
What for?
a [ ] for the 30 necklaces
b [ ] for the small piece of jewelry
c [ ] for sightseeing

6 "I will take you to a cash machine."
Who said this?
a [ ] Brad b [ ] Jay c [ ] Viki

c Write about a good or bad experience you've had on vacation. Remember to include:

- where you were
- what happened
- who you met.

Review and extension

1 GRAMMAR

Correct the sentences.

1 By the time we got to his house, the party finished.
By the time we got to his house, the party had finished.
2 I said her that she couldn't go to the beach by herself.
3 He told me that my mother has called earlier that day.
4 We told that her father wouldn't buy her a new computer.
5 Tom never rode a camel before, so he was pretty nervous.
6 Our train has already left when we finally arrived at the station.

2 VOCABULARY

Correct the sentences.

1 I had a great time at your party on Saturday. It was really funny.
I had a great time at your party on Saturday. It was really fun.
2 She's a really onest person. If sales assistants give her too much change, she always tells them.
3 He's very easy going. I'm sure he won't mind if you bring your friend with you when you go to his house for dinner.
4 I'm not a very confidant person. For example, I don't like speaking when I'm in a meeting with a large group of people.
5 Teachers have to learn to be patent with their students because sometimes they don't learn things immediately.
6 Why are you always so carless? You've already lost your cell phone twice this year!

3 WORDPOWER *age*

Underline the correct words to complete the sentences.

1 My father's 48 this year, so he's definitely *of middle age* / *middle aged* / *in the middle of age*.
2 *At your age* / *In your age* / *On your age*, I was working 12 hours a day in a factory.
3 It's really important for young people to save money for their *older age* / *old age* / *third age*.
4 They're sisters who are only 18 months *different of age* / *apart in age* / *age difference*.
5 I learned to read *at an early age* / *of early age* / *at young age* – I could read when I was only three.
6 He's *near my age* / *old like me* / *about my age* – we both went to college at the same time.

REVIEW YOUR PROGRESS

Look again at Review Your Progress on p. 126 of the Student's Book. How well can you do these things now?
3 = very well 2 = well 1 = not so well

I CAN ...	
tell a story	[ ]
talk about family relationships	[ ]
agree and disagree in discussions	[ ]
write a short story.	[ ]

Unit 1

01.01

1 bank
2 awful
3 perfect
4 music
5 ugly
6 hotel
7 often
8 arrive
9 university
10 favorite

01.02

MEGAN What's Andrea doing in that store?
NAOMI She's buying some postcards to send to her family.
M Really? I don't usually send postcards. I usually write a message on Facebook. And sometimes I post a few photos of my vacation on Instagram.
N Yes, me too, but Andrea's grandparents don't use social media, so she sends them postcards instead.
M Oh, and what are Marco and Jack doing this morning?
N They're spending the day at the beach.
M But Marco doesn't like swimming in the ocean. He says the water's too cold.
N Yes, but it's really hot today!

01.03

SAM Hi, James! Long time no see! How are you?
JAMES Hi, Sam. I'm fine, thanks. What a nice surprise! Great to see you!
S Yes, it's really nice to see you, too.
J Where are you living these days?
S Oh, not far from here. On Park Road, near the baseball stadium.
J Oh, how nice!
S And this is my wife, Jess.
J Your wife – wow! That's wonderful news! Nice to meet you, Jess.
JESS Nice to meet you, too.

01.04

1 Sea View Road? Oh, how nice!
2 Your husband – wow! That's wonderful news!
3 I really need to go. I'm late.
4 What a nice surprise!
5 Say hello to Carlos for me.
6 Long time no see!
7 It was really nice to meet you.
8 I'll give you a call.
9 It was great to see you again.
10 When did we last see each other?

01.05

1 I'm pretty sure it was two months ago.
2 What a nice surprise!
3 It was really nice to meet you.
4 I'm sorry, but I really need to go.
5 Where are you living these days?
6 I'm late for a meeting.

01.06

PRESENTER When you move to a new school or town or start college, it's important to make new friends. But it's not easy. On today's, show new students at Princeton University tell us how they are making friends during the first few weeks of school. First up is Carson.
CARSON I don't particularly like going to parties, and I hardly ever go out at night, so it was difficult for me to make friends. I like people who I have something in common with, so I joined the school hiking club. We meet every Sunday and usually go for a hike in the forests or by the river near the school. It's a lot of fun, and I talk to all kinds of people.
Pr Joining a club is a great way to meet new people. But there are other ways. Let's hear from Sophia, a 19-year-old student.
SOPHIA I'm studying acting, so I like talking to people. I'm not particularly interested in joining a club because I usually prefer to meet people who like a lot of different things. I posted a message on an online student group saying, "I'm looking for some friends. No rude or serious people. We can meet for coffee in the students' café every Tuesday." About ten people come each week. It's a lot of fun, and everyone is different.
Pr But if you don't want to start your own group, there are other ways. Over to Luis.
LUIS I don't really like using social media to make friends. I'm living in a large student house with about 30 other people, so the first week I knocked on everyone's bedroom door and said hello. Everyone here is friendly. Now I'm rarely on my own, and there is often someone to talk to or go out with at night.

Unit 2

02.01

depart	departed	look	looked
love	loved	post	posted
listen	listened	invite	invited
hate	hated	enjoy	enjoyed
sound	sounded	like	liked

02.02

1 Were you waiting for the bus?
2 I wasn't driving the car.
3 They were watching TV.
4 We weren't having dinner.
5 She was talking on her phone.
6 Was she listening?
7 He wasn't smoking.
8 They weren't playing chess.

02.03

1 Is there anything else I can help you with?
2 Could you tell me where the information desk is?
3 How much is a round-trip ticket to Boston?
4 How often do the buses leave for the airport?
5 What time is the next train to Barcelona?
6 Can I pay for my ticket in dollars?
7 Where can I buy a sandwich for the trip?
8 How much does it cost to get a taxi to the airport?

02.04

A Excuse me.
B Yes, how can I help you?
A Could you tell me which platform the next train to Chicago leaves from?
B Of course. It leaves from platform 2.
A OK, thanks. And what time does it leave?
B It leaves at 10:32, in 12 minutes.
A Great. Thanks.
B Is there anything else I can help you with?
A Actually, there is one more thing. Where can I buy some coffee? Is there a café near here?
B Yes, there is. There's a café on the platform, over there.
A Great. Thanks so much.
B No problem. Have a good trip.

02.05

1 When did you check into your hotel?
2 How can I help you?
3 Did you get a visa when you went to China?
4 What time did your plane take off?
5 What time is your train?
6 How much is a round-trip ticket to Bogotá?

02.06

GEORGE And now we go over to Sara with today's traffic and travel news. I hear it is particularly bad on highways 75 and 85?
SARA Thanks, George, that's right. The heavy rain this morning caused problems on 85. Four cars hit each other and because of that, there were long delays between Atlanta and the airport. It doesn't look very good on 75. A truck broke down near Hapeville about three hours ago, and there was a huge traffic jam half an hour later. Peter from East Point just texted on eight-seven-six-six-three to say that there is a long line of cars now. So if you need to get to Hapeville this evening, you might want to get off the highway and go on Metropolitan Parkway.
Highway 20 is looking a lot better today. There were no delays when I last checked, which is great for anyone who is going to the annual fall festival at Sweetwater Creek State Park tomorrow. If you're driving there, look for parking before the festival. There will be signs. However, police warn not to park your car and walk on the side of the highway.
Unusually, there aren't many problems on the subway today, but if you are going away this weekend, a lot of subway lines aren't working normally, so check before you go.
If you are flying from Hartsfield-Jackson International Airport, please call your airline before you go. The computer systems at the airport weren't working this morning and many flights were canceled today. The computers are working now, but there are long delays and even longer lines! James and Fatima called to say their flight to India was delayed by over 12 hours, and they had to check into a hotel by the airport for the night. But I'm happy to say that they've boarded their plane now and are on their way.
G Well, I hope they have a visa or they'll have another long line when they arrive!
S I hope so, too! It sounds like they're going to have a real adventure. Back to you, George.
G Thanks, Sara. And here's the latest song by …

Unit 3

03.01

A Good morning. Can I help you?
B Um, yes. I'm looking for a present for my mother.
A Are you looking for anything in particular?
B Well, she loves earrings.
A Really? How about these earrings? They're really beautiful. A perfect present …
B Do you have anything cheaper?
A Well, these earrings here are cheaper. They're only $30 with the discount.
B Mm, I think she'd like them. On second thought, maybe I should get something else.
A OK. Um, let me see … what about this necklace?
B Yes, it's beautiful. OK, I'll take it.

03.02

1 Can you show us something else?
2 Can you enter your PIN, please?
3 I'm looking for a present for my husband.
4 Do you have any black jeans?
5 Thanks. I'll take it.
6 Actually, I think we should buy her a book.

03.03

DJ And now it's time for today's talking point. What's the nicest thing you have ever done for someone? Have you given something expensive away to someone or just made someone smile? Call, text, or email me now. First on is Anita from Wilmington.
ANITA Hello, Baz. My neighbor doesn't have a job right now, and it's her daughter's 13th birthday today. I know she couldn't afford to have a party, so I thought I could help.
DJ And what have you done?
A I've borrowed a speaker from my brother and some disco lights from my friend. And we've turned part of her backyard into a beach with umbrellas and beach chairs. A lot of the neighbors have made food, and we're going to have a beach party and disco this evening.
DJ That must have made your neighbor smile. Thanks for your call, Anita, and have a great night. What a nice woman. Next we have Gary from Silver Lake. What's the nicest thing you've done?

GARY Hi, Baz. Last year I was downtown when a tourist asked me how to get to the museum. I gave him directions, and then we started talking. He was from Colombia, and he was really friendly. Then it started raining really hard. He didn't have a jacket, so I lent him my umbrella. I asked him to bring it to my office when he was leaving Silver Lake, and then I forgot about it. Four days later, he brought it to my office. I didn't expect that. We went and got coffee together. We got along well and we became friends. When he left, he invited me to visit him in Colombia next December. I've been saving up all year, and I've just booked my ticket. I can't wait!

DJ That's a great story, Gary. Enjoy your vacation! Before we go, I've gotten an email from Mike in Darwin. He has started a group called "Give someone a hug, make someone smile." Every Sunday, he walks around downtown with his friends, giving people hugs and hopefully making them smile. Good luck with that, Mike – and be careful!

Unit 4

04.01

A So what have you planned for this evening?
B Well, my parents are arriving at the station on the 5:30 train from Trenton.
A So, are you meeting them at the station?
B Yes, we are. We're taking a taxi from our house at 5:00.
A Good. So where are they staying?
B At the Hilton Hotel. They have a double room with a balcony.
A Great. And what about the restaurant?
B I've reserved a table for eight at seven o'clock. Everyone's coming to the restaurant at 6:45 so we can all be there when they arrive.
A Fantastic. Have you told the restaurant that it's your father's birthday?
B Yes, they've made him a special cake with *Happy 60th* on it. They're bringing it to our table at nine o'clock, together with the coffee.
A And what about tomorrow?
B They're not flying to Chicago until the afternoon, so there's plenty of time. Their flight's at 3:30.
A Great, so it's all arranged. I have to go now because I'm meeting Sally for coffee in ten minutes. See you later!

04.02

1 Are you going to go out tonight?
2 What are you going to do for your birthday?
3 He's not going to take a vacation this year.
4 We're going to try to find a taxi.
5 I'm going to take a shower after breakfast.
6 They're not going to do their homework.
7 She's going to call her brother.
8 I'm not going to go to Cancún this year.

04.03

1 We want to go swimming today.
2 They won't take you to the old mansion.
3 I won't go to that restaurant again.
4 You want to wait for the next bus.
5 I want to study English again next year.
6 Felipe and I won't invite him to our party.

04.04

A Are you doing anything on Wednesday? Would you like to get coffee?
B Oh, that sounds nice. Let me check my phone. No, sorry, I can't do Wednesday. I'm going shopping with my mom.
A Oh, OK. How about Friday? Is that OK for you?
B Friday … hang on a minute … no, sorry. I'm going to Seattle for the day. This week's really busy for me.
A OK, so you can't do this week. What are you doing next Monday?
B Next Monday? Let me check. Nothing! I can do next Monday.
A Great! So we can meet for coffee on Monday?
B Yes, Monday's fine. Where should we go?
A Should we meet at the Coffee Place at 11:00?
B Perfect! Eleven o'clock. See you then.

04.05

1 How about that new French café?
2 Are you doing anything this Saturday?
3 This week's really busy for us.
4 What time should we come over?
5 What are you doing next Tuesday?
6 Would you like to come over for lunch?
7 I can't do Thursday this week.
8 Is this Sunday OK for you?

04.06

1 I can't meet you tomorrow.
2 He can meet us at the station.
3 I didn't understand him.
4 She hasn't seen that movie.
5 I have to start cooking dinner.
6 They don't like basketball.

04.07

ISAAC What are your plans when you finish college this summer, Marlon?
MARLON Well, my brother Alex is getting married in July.
I That's great news. Where is the wedding?
M His fiancée, Laura, is Italian, so it's going to be in her town in Tuscany in this magnificent old church there. The town is really pretty.
I That sounds wonderful. Is it going to be a big wedding?
M The party is in the town hall, which is huge. Laura has a really big family.
I Do you have to do anything at the wedding?
M Yeah, I'm going to read a poem I wrote.
I Great! That's exciting. I guess you're going to need a new suit for that.
M Yes, I have to look my best, especially in front of all those Italian guests.
I Really?
M Yes, they always look really nice. My dad's going to buy me a new suit if I do well in school. Something really nice.
I Great! Can you speak any Italian?
M *Si. Un po'!* But I'm starting classes next week. The Italian guy in our class, Gavino, is teaching me.
I That's a good idea. How long are you going to Italy for?
M I'm going for two weeks. I'm flying to Rome with my parents on July 14, and we're going to go sightseeing for a few days. My mom wants to see all the ancient buildings.
I I love Rome. You can walk down a street of really cool modern buildings, then turn a corner and see something that's 2,000 years old. It's amazing.
M Wow, I can't wait to go.
I Anyway, I have to go. I'm going on a date tonight, and I want to go to the hairdresser's before it closes.
M OK, well, make sure you shave before you meet her, Isaac.
I Don't worry, I will. See you tomorrow.
M OK, see you then.

Unit 5

05.01

1 Should I lend you some money for the bus?
2 Maybe you should ask your manager for the day off.
3 I'll look up the train times online.
4 Do you want me to call a taxi for our guest?
5 Why don't I drive you to the airport?
6 How about arranging a meeting in Mexico City?
7 Why don't you borrow some money from your dad?
8 You could catch a direct flight to Quebec.

05.02

1 **A** Should I book a room for your meeting?
B Yes, good idea.
2 **A** Would you like me to drive you to the bus station?
B No, I'll be fine. Don't worry about it. I can walk.
3 **A** But you won't be able to have any lunch.
B Oh, never mind. I'm not really hungry.
4 **A** I'm really sorry. I can't go to the movies tonight.
B Oh, it doesn't matter. We can go another time.
5 How about asking your boss if you can have more time for the report?
6 Why don't I book the train tickets online?
7 Maybe you should invite your boss to the meeting, too?
8 You could send her some flowers for her birthday.

05.03

1 Would you like some coffee?
2 Yes, I would. Thanks.
3 Could you help me with my report?
4 Yes, of course I could.
5 You should get a taxi.
6 Yes, you're right. I should.
7 Should you book a meeting room?
8 Well, what do you think? Should I?

05.04

INTERVIEWER Thank you for coming in, Josh. First of all, I'd like to talk about your résumé. You have some good qualifications, but you've had a lot of different jobs in the last five years. Can you talk about those?
JOSH Yes, I worked as a construction worker when I finished college. I enjoyed being outside and getting exercise, but I had to work many hours every day and start early in the morning, which I hated, so I decided to look for other jobs.
I So, you don't like working long hours then. Hmm. Tell me about your next job. You worked as a hairdresser, didn't you?
J Yes, I did. I learned a lot of skills while I was there, and I really liked the place. But I didn't like having to talk to people every day. I had to talk to the customers and make coffee.
I Hmm. OK. What about your last job? You were an IT worker.
J Yes, that was great. I earned a good salary, and I worked with a nice team of people. Sometimes when we were busy, I had to work on weekends, which wasn't great, but I usually just worked Monday to Friday. I didn't have to work with people so much, and I could often just sit at my desk and use the Internet, when we weren't busy, of course. And my manager didn't mind what time I started work.
I And what time did you usually start work?
J The latest I could start was 10:30 a.m.
I OK, Josh, so why would you like to work as a bank teller for Bank One?
J I'd like to work on a team and get some good experience working in a bank. It looks like a nice environment to work in. And it pays really well, too.
I But you don't like working hard or dealing with people every day. Those are important parts of the job.
J Well, …
I I'm sorry, Josh, but I don't think you're what we're looking for. Thanks for coming in today and good luck.
J Oh. OK. I thought this would be a good job for me.
I I don't think so. But good luck with your search. Thank you.
J Thank you.

Unit 6

06.01

1 We took my grandma to the theater.
2 The children wanted to go to the zoo.
3 Where did you lose your cell phone?
4 Would you like some coffee?
5 Who did you invite to the party?
6 I don't think you should go to work today.
7 Could I borrow $5, please?
8 What did you think of the food?

06.02

1 **A** I think it's a good idea to reserve a table. The restaurant might be full.
B Yes, I guess so. Saturday night can be very busy.
2 **A** Someone stole my bag when I was at the beach this afternoon.
B How awful! I'm really sorry to hear that.
3 **A** I'd talk to your boss about it.
B I don't think I should do that. She'll be mad at me.
4 **A** I wouldn't worry too much. You can get a new passport at the embassy.
B Yes, you're right. I can go there one day next week.
5 **A** Do you think I should invite Jorge to the surprise party?
B No, I don't think that's a very good idea. Anna doesn't like him very much.

6 **A** What do you think I should do?
B I think you should go to the police station.
7 **A** I didn't get the job in marketing.
B Oh, that's too bad. I'm sure you'll get another job soon.
8 **A** I broke my finger on Saturday.
B Oh, that's a shame. So that means you can't play tennis today?

06.03

1 Which job do you think I should apply for?
2 I think you should ask your coworkers.
3 I'm really sorry to hear that.
4 Do you think I should look for a new job?
5 I think it's a good idea to talk to your boss.
6 I'd talk to your parents about it.
7 I wouldn't apply for the new marketing job.
8 I don't think you should leave your job.

06.04

1 You're from Canada, right?
2 Elena works at the Spanish Embassy.
3 Would you like to work in Houston?
4 We're having a surprise party for Anna.
5 My boss wants to talk to me.

06.05

MADISON Hi, Elena. How are you?
ELENA Hi, Madison. Not so good. I'm getting really annoyed with my little brother Jacob at the moment. I'm trying to study for my exams, and he keeps interrupting me. Sometimes he listens to his music very loud late at night. Sometimes he borrows something from me that I need to study, like my headphones or laptop. I can't concentrate on my work for more than a few minutes. It's awful.
MAD You should go and study in the library. It's really quiet there, and you won't have to deal with the interruptions. I go there most weekends to study.
MAX You shouldn't have to go somewhere else. Ask your parents to deal with your brother. Your exams are more important than your brother. Your parents understand that.
E That's a good idea, Max. I'll ask my dad for help tonight. My brother will listen to him. And I'll also think about going to the library this weekend. It's nice to have a change sometimes when you're studying. How's your studying going, Max?
MAX My problem is, I just can't remember anything from history. I read a page, and then ten minutes later I've forgotten it.
MAD That's not unusual. You should try writing down what you've just read. It's amazing how much more you will remember that way.
E And you should also record yourself reading your notes out loud, and then you can listen to them on your phone. You'll be surprised how much you can remember.
MAX Yes, I'll definitely try those ideas.
E Sometimes I even sing my notes. It's a little embarrassing, but it will help you remember a lot of information.
MAX That's a great idea.
MAD Any advice to help me understand physics? It's so confusing. I look at it, I can read it, I can remember it, but when I think about it, I just don't understand it.
E It doesn't sound like physics is your subject, Madison. Maybe you should try something else!
MAX That's not very nice, Elena. I'm really interested in physics. I'd be happy to help you with it if you like, Madison. I think you just need someone to explain it to you.
MAD Thanks, Max. I think that Elena might be right, but I really want to pass the physics exam this year, so I don't have to do it again next year. Are you free this weekend?
MAX No, I'm afraid not. I need to record all my history notes on my phone!

Unit 7

07.01

1 **A** So, what's the problem?
B I have a stomachache. It's really painful.
2 **A** When did this start?
B About two days ago.
3 **A** Where does it hurt? Can you show me?
B Here, in this area.
4 **A** Can I take a look? So, does it hurt here?
B Yes, it does. It hurts all the time. I can't get to sleep.
5 **A** Are you taking anything for the pain?
B Yes, I've taken some ibuprofen.
6 **A** Well, I don't think it's anything to worry about.
B Phew! That's good to hear.
7 **A** I think it's just indigestion.
B Just indigestion? What a relief!
8 **A** I'll give you a prescription for some medicine. Take two pills every four hours.
B OK. Thank you, Doctor.

07.02

1 Don't worry. It's nothing to worry about.
2 Phew! That's good to hear.
3 It hurts all the time. I can't get to sleep.
4 Can I take a look?
5 Are you taking anything for the pain?
6 I feel sick and exhausted.
7 I think you need to see another doctor.
8 So, what's the problem?
9 What a relief!
10 You shouldn't stay in bed.

07.03

1 Do you exercise?
2 When did this problem start?
3 Could you have a few tests tomorrow?
4 How much ibuprofen have you taken?
5 How long have you had this problem?
6 Are you taking anything for the pain?
7 Do you have any allergies?
8 Have you had any accidents recently?

07.04

ORGANIZER Welcome to the Lindfield School Reunion – a chance for students who finished school 20 years ago to meet again. It's great to see so many of our old classmates here, and I hope you all have a great evening. Dinner will be …
SEAN Wow, I haven't seen some of these people for at least 20 years. It's funny to see how everyone has changed.
SARAH I know. I was just talking to Nick Downes. Do you remember him? He used to be really good looking. He was the most popular boy in our class.
SE Yes, I remember Nick. Is that him over there?
SA Yes. He's put on a lot of weight, hasn't he? Apparently, he just got divorced from Jenny Wang. She wanted him to go on a diet and give up smoking and drinking coffee. But you know Nick – he never liked doing what he was told.
SE Yes, I remember! So he hasn't changed that much then. Who's that attractive thin woman he's talking to? Isn't it Lisa Baker?
SA Yes, I was talking to her earlier. She used to be really overweight, didn't she? She was telling me that she went on a diet and started getting fit about ten years ago. She's a lot more confident now and a lot healthier. She's just gotten engaged to a man from Germany.
SE That's really good to hear. I used to get along well with Lisa.
SA Have you seen Mike Andrews yet? You know, little Mike. He used to be poor and drove a really old car.
SE Yes, of course.
SA He arrived in a brand-new sports car. He started a computer company and got rich. That's him talking to Kristina Martinez, Emma Alexander, and Rachel Anastasio.
SE Wow! He looks great. And he seems to be a lot more popular than he used to be!
SA Ha, yes. Oh, wow. Look who's just arrived! It's Brian Ramirez. With Nicole Aydin.
SE Yes, I saw they'd gotten together on Facebook. It's funny. They used to hate each other.
SA I know. They used to fight all the time. They look really happy now.
SE Yeah. Oh, and what about Martin Dowd? Is he coming? I remember you used to really like him.
SA Yes, he was very popular. I got in touch with him last month to see if he was going to come. Unfortunately, he couldn't. He's getting married this weekend.
SE Again? Is that his third marriage?
SA Yes, that's right. Well, he used to have a lot of girlfriends at school. I think he went out with five of the girls in our class.
SE Well, some people never change.
SA Yes, that's true.
O And now, ladies and gentlemen, please take your seats for dinner.

Unit 8

08.01

play squash	go snowboarding	do gymnastics
play golf	go ice skating	do yoga
play volleyball	go jogging	do track and field
play tennis	go rock climbing	do aerobics
play basketball	go skateboarding	do karate
play soccer	go scuba diving	do judo
play ice hockey	go windsurfing	
go surfing		

08.02

1 snowboarding
2 windsurfing
3 jogging
4 gymnastics
5 ice hockey

08.03

1 I meant to send you an email, …
2 I'm sorry I didn't come to your party.
3 I couldn't call you last night …
4 I had to stay late at work yesterday.
5 Sorry, I didn't mean to make you worry.
6 I was going to call you, …
7 I'm sorry I didn't reply to your message, …
8 I had to visit my grandma yesterday.

08.04

1 I meant to send you an email, but my computer wasn't working.
2 I'm sorry I didn't come to your party.
3 I couldn't call you last night because my phone was dead.
4 I had to stay late at work yesterday.
5 Sorry, I didn't mean to make you worry.
6 I was going to call you, but I couldn't find your number.
7 I'm sorry I didn't reply to your message, but I've been really busy for the last two days.
8 I had to visit my grandma yesterday.

08.05

MATT Now on Riverside Radio it's time for our weekly guide to what's going on this weekend. As usual, we're going to talk to four listeners with very different interests about what they recommend doing this weekend. First of all, we'll talk to Rachel from Albany.
RACHEL Hi, Matt. There's a lot happening this weekend if you like outdoor sports. Rock climbing at the Stirling Ranges has started again for the year. All of the climbing routes have been included in the new guidebook, which can be bought only at the information center. But be careful! This is only for experienced climbers. But if water is more your thing, then the Margaret River Surfers will be out on the water somewhere in the area. Where they meet depends on the waves, but all the information you need is on their website.
M Thanks, Rachel. That sounds like a lot of fun. Let's talk to Gareth now in Perth.
GARETH Hi, Matt. If you're interested in Italy and art, there's the Italian Arts Festival. It includes movies which have been directed by many of Italy's greatest directors, and if you go to the art gallery, you can also see photographs of the actors taken by the directors. The movies will be shown at the Luna Palace Movie Theater.
M Thanks a lot, Gareth. Let's talk to Carolina now in Fremantle. What's your weekend looking like?
CAROLINA It's all about the written word in Fremantle this weekend. The annual poetry festival, which has been going on for ten years, returns. As usual, the festival has been organized by the Fremantle Young Poets Society and includes something for everyone. The highlight this year is the performance of "bush poetry" by a group of young poets, to music performed by local folk musicians, The Western Arc, on the beach at Wilson Park, south of Fremantle.

M A beach I've been to many times and a great place to hear some beautiful music and poetry. Finally, let's talk to Jenny in Bunbury. What's happening in Bunbury this weekend?

JENNY Well, it's time to get active in Bunbury this weekend. It's the annual 10-km race on Sunday. I've been training for the last three months for this, so I'm really looking forward to it. But if you haven't done any training, you're still welcome. Over 1,000 people will be running, jogging, or walking, and I'm sure everyone will enjoy the race, which was won last year by local athlete Jack Harding. It starts at 10 a.m.

M Well, good luck with that, Jenny. I hope you have a great time. I might come along to support you. So, it sounds like there are a lot of things to do this weekend, for people who want to get active, and for those who prefer to get their brains working. I hope you've heard something that you're interested in doing and, most of all, I hope you have a great weekend.

Unit 9

09.01

1 I enjoy studying math in school, but I hate taking exams.
2 If you take notes in class, it will be easier to study for the exam.
3 I'm going to work harder next year, so that I get better grades.
4 If she fails her exam, she'll have to take it again in January.
5 Although he got excellent grades, he didn't get accepted to Oxford University.

09.02

A Is it possible to speak to Becky Yu, please?
B Of course. I'll transfer you to her office.
C Hello, Becky Yu's office.
A Oh, hello. Is Becky there, please?
C No, I'm afraid she's not available. She's in a meeting. Can I take a message?
A Yes, OK. Can you tell her that I called?
C Yes, of course. Who's calling, please?
A This is Paul Roberts speaking.
C OK. Would you like her to call you back?
A Yes, please. I'm here all morning.
C Does she have your number?
A Yes, she does.
C Great. I'll ask her to call you back.
A Thanks. Bye.

09.03

AMY Oh, hello, is this Rob?
ROB Yes, it is.
A Hi, it's Amy.
R Oh, hi, Amy.
A Is now a good time to talk?
R Well, I'm a little busy.
A Sorry, Rob. I didn't catch that.
R Yes, I was just saying that I'm busy. Sorry, but I have a meeting in five minutes. Can I call you back?
A Sure. Is everything OK?
R Yes, everything's fine, but I need to go.
A OK. Call me when you have time.
R Talk to you soon. Bye.
A Bye.

09.04

1 The movie starts at 8:50.
The movie starts at 8:15.
2 We're catching the nine o'clock bus.
We're catching the ten o'clock bus.
3 My new boyfriend's name is James.
My new boyfriend's name is John.
4 The show is on channel 11.
The show is on channel seven.
5 We're leaving for vacation on Tuesday.
We're leaving for vacation on Thursday.
6 I was born in 1990.
I was born in 1991.

09.05

PROFESSOR Good morning, Roberto. Thanks for coming to see me this morning.
ROBERTO Good morning, Professor Ryan.
P I'd like to talk to you about your work. There seems to be a few problems.
R Problems, Professor Ryan?
P Yes. The last two essays that you wrote for me were pretty bad. I really don't think that you read any of the books. And you handed them both in late. I know that you're very busy at the moment, but so is everyone, and all the other students managed to do the essays on time.
R I'm sorry. I had six essays to write this semester.
P I know that you just finished high school last year, but when you start a degree in psychology, that's how it is. If your next essay is late, I will refuse to grade it. OK?
R Yes, I understand.
P You've also avoided coming to my class for the last two weeks. If you don't come to class, you won't learn anything, Roberto. This is really important. Do you not like listening to my lectures, or do you have something better to do?
R No, of course not. I really regret not coming, but I was sick. But one of the other students agreed to lend me his notes.
P OK. Well, I recommend reading them very carefully. And if you don't understand something, come and talk to me. There are exams at the end of this course, and if you don't attend every lecture, there is a good chance that you will fail.
R Yes, I know. I've started studying for them already.
P Well, that's good news. I've arranged to meet a group of students every Wednesday afternoon to talk about the exam. I think it would be very useful for you to join us.
G Yes, that sounds really useful. Unfortunately, I play soccer every Wednesday. Soccer is very important to me, Professor Ryan.
P And your degree isn't?
R Yes, that is very important, too. Of course.
P Only 25 students get accepted every year to study psychology at this university. You are very lucky to be here. If your work doesn't get better, you may have to leave the program. I want you to think very carefully about what is most important to you.
R I will. Thank you.
P Do you have any questions that you want to ask me?
R Yes, there is something. Which books should I read?
P The books on the reading list.
R Which list is that?
P The list that I gave you at the start of the class.
R I don't think I have it.
P So, you haven't read any of the books then.
R Uh, no, I haven't.

Unit 10

10.01

1 If I had a lot of money, I would buy an expensive sports car.
2 Would you marry him if he didn't live so far away?
3 If I were you, I wouldn't go swimming in the ocean today.
4 If he asked her to go to Argentina with him, she probably would.
5 I would come and stay with you in New York if the flights weren't so expensive.
6 She wouldn't have to drive to work every day if she lived closer to her office.

10.02

1 decision
2 enjoyment
3 complaint
4 description
5 explanation
6 delivery
7 describe
8 complain

10.03

CUSTOMER Good morning. Could you help me, please?
SALES ASSISTANT Yes, of course. How can I help?
C I'd like to return this speaker, please.
SA Would you like to exchange it for something else?
C No, I'd just like a refund, please.
SA Do you have a receipt?
C No, I'm sorry, I don't. It was a present from my boyfriend, but the sound quality is very bad.
SA Well, I'm terribly sorry, but we don't give refunds without a receipt.
C Could I speak to the manager, please?
SA Yes, of course. I'll go and get him.
MANAGER What seems to be the problem?
C I'd like to make a complaint.

10.04

1 Excuse me, but this isn't what I ordered.
2 I'll ask someone to look at that for you right away.
3 We've been here for over an hour, but we still haven't ordered.
4 These shoes don't fit me because they're a little small.
5 I've changed my mind, and I've decided to keep it.
6 I'd like to exchange it for something else.
7 I'd like to return this watch, please.
8 I'll give you a full refund.
9 Your sales assistant hasn't been very helpful.

10.05

1 Can you bring us the check, please?
2 Would you like me to give you a refund?
3 Did you bring your receipt with you?
4 Where did you buy it?
5 Could you wait a moment, please?
6 Can you take our order now, please?
7 Can I exchange these jeans for another pair?
8 Could you call the manager, please?

10.06

ZUZA Haluk, you buy a lot of things online, don't you?
HALUK Yes, I do. I think it's really convenient and usually much cheaper than going to a store. You can go shopping when you feel like it, and there are no lines to deal with. I'd do all my shopping online if I could.
Z And never leave your house! What I don't like is that you have to wait a few days for what you've bought to be delivered. That makes me think twice about buying online.
H That's true, but you don't have to wait too long. Usually it arrives in one or two days.
Z What was the last thing you bought online?
H I bought a new coat last week.
Z I would never buy clothes online. You can't try them on.
H I saw a photo of the coat, and there was also a description of it.
Z And were you happy with it when it arrived?
H Not really. It was the wrong size. It was too small for me, and the color was different from the photo. The description wasn't very good either. The website said that it was a leather coat, but I don't think it is.
Z Did you complain?
H Yes, I wrote an email to the company and asked for a refund.
Z And what happened?
H They haven't replied yet.
Z Hmm. Well, if I were you, I'd call them up and ask for a refund, and an explanation, too.
H Yes, I'll do that next week. I'm sure it'll be fine.
Z I wouldn't keep on using that company, though. Have you had any other problems buying things online?
H A few. Occasionally things break in the mail. And sometimes the mail carrier isn't careful with something. I bought a book a few weeks ago, and when it arrived, it was completely wet. I think the mail carrier had dropped it in some water. But it's usually fine. I buy a lot of books and presents online. It's great because you can find absolutely everything. There's so much more choice than at the local bookstore.
Z Yes, but I enjoy looking around the bookstore. It's really enjoyable.
H Me too. Sometimes I find the book in the store and then buy it online! It's often a lot cheaper.
Z Hmm, but if everyone did that, there wouldn't be any more bookstores or stores of any kind! That would be awful.
H I don't think that would happen.
Z It's happening right now. A lot of stores have closed down in our town because people shop online.
H Well, I'm going to keep on shopping online.
Z And I'm going to keep on going to the stores. It's fun, sociable, and who knows, I might meet someone interesting at the bookstore. If you went shopping more, you might meet someone, too. You certainly won't meet anyone sitting at home on your computer.

Unit 11

11.01

1	mountain climbing	5	bread knife
2	computer screen	6	parking lot
3	science fiction	7	coffee cup
4	address book	8	bookshelf

11.02

A Good morning. Please take a seat. I'll be with you in a moment … Now, how can I help you?
B Could you help us find a hotel in Miami, please?
A Yes, of course. Would you like a hotel in South Beach?
B Yes, if possible.
A OK, how about Paradise Hotel? They have some available rooms.
B Do they have free parking?
A Yes, they do, but you can walk to all the great places! It's about a five-minute walk to Ocean Drive. And it's across the street from the beach. It's one of the nicest hotels in all of Miami.
B Great. Can you ask if they have a double room for three nights? And can you check the price?
A Yes, sure. I'm afraid hotels in Miami are really expensive. A lot of people think that Miami's the most expensive beach city for tourists in the U.S.
B Yes, the hotel that we stayed in last year cost over $300 a night!
A OK, I've booked it for you. If you're coming from the highway, go down Alton Road and make a left on 7th Street. It's on the left, across from the beach.
B Great. Thank you very much.

11.03

1	accidentally	6	surprisingly
2	on purpose	7	amazingly
3	by chance	8	fortunately
4	unfortunately	9	as expected
5	luckily		

11.04

A Can you tell me where the Lincoln Meeting Room is?
B Yes, sure. It's on the second floor. Go through that door over there. Then go down to the end of the corridor. Then go up the stairs to the second floor. At the top of the stairs, turn left and go down another corridor. The Lincoln Room is the fourth door on the right.
A Great, thanks.

11.05

1 Go down the stairs to the first floor.
2 Go through those doors and then down the corridor.
3 So, first go down the corridor to the stairs?
4 Could you tell me where the staff lounge is, please?
5 Then go down the corridor, and it's the first office on the right.
6 Go up the stairs to the third floor.
7 So, can I just check?
8 OK, I think I got it.
9 At the top of the stairs, turn right and go down another corridor.
10 The meeting room is the second door on the left.

11.06

1	bird	3	air	5	worst	7	sir
2	fur	4	where	6	bear	8	fair

11.07

REPORTER Police are looking for two men who stole money from a cash machine outside Western Bank on Harris Road here in Reno at midnight last night. The men arrived at the bank in a large car and crashed into the cash machine on purpose four times. Monica Edwards is the woman who saw what happened.
MONICA I live across from the bank and was in bed at the back of my apartment. But just before midnight, I got up to go to the bathroom. When I heard a car going very fast, I went into the living room and looked out the front window. I've never seen anything like it. The car drove up to the cash machine at about 50 miles per hour and didn't stop. I thought it was an accident, but amazingly, they did it again and again. I called the police immediately.
R What did the men do next?
M They got out of the car, put on some gloves, and tried to break the cash machine open with a baseball bat, which they got from the back of the car. Fortunately, they couldn't open it, but then the driver got back into the car and drove into the machine again.
R Can you describe the men?
M Yes, I can. Fortunately, there were streetlights on, so it was easy to see them. The man who was driving the car was about 20 years old, very tall, and with very short hair. The other man was about the same age, was short, and had dark hair, a hat, and sunglasses.
R Um … how long did it take them to get the cash machine open?
M Unfortunately, the second time the machine broke, and they could steal some money. Luckily, the police also arrived at this time, so the men managed to take only a small amount of money. They quickly jumped back into the car and tried to drive off. But they drove backward into a road sign, and then, unsurprisingly, the car didn't start because it was so damaged. So they got out and ran away down Park Avenue.
R Did the police go after them?
M Yes, the police car followed them, but the men ran into the park and disappeared.
R I hear that you found something nearby.
M Yes, I found a key ring with the name Terry on it and a house key. It was next to the car. I think one of the men dropped it. I gave it to the police when they came back.
R And what about the car?
M The police think that the men stole it from a parking lot earlier in the day.
R Thank you, Mrs. Edwards. Photos of the two men which were taken by security cameras outside the bank will be on the TV show *Everyday Criminals* on channel 7 tonight at 8. And now, over to Adam with today's sports news.

Unit 12

12.01

brought	talked	run	woken
come	known	taught	won
done	spoken		

12.02

1 **A** I believe yoga is a great way to relax before you go to bed.
B You're absolutely right. I try and do a few exercises every night.
2 **A** I think Brazil has the best soccer team in the world.
B I'm not sure about that. I think Argentina will beat them in the final.
3 **A** In my opinion, Venice is a more attractive city than Florence.
B That could be. It's such a beautiful place to visit. I love it!
4 **A** This is a nicer movie theater than the one we went to last week.
B I agree. The seats are very comfortable, and the screen is wider.
5 **A** Barcelona is the biggest city in Spain.
B I don't think so. I think there are more people in Madrid, actually.
6 **A** Leonardo DiCaprio is a better actor than Brad Pitt.
B That's true. He was amazing in *The Revenant*.
7 **A** In my opinion, Italian coffee is better than French coffee.
B I'm sorry, but how do you know? You don't drink coffee!
8 **A** I think the weather in the U.K. in winter is much better than in Germany.
B I'm afraid I don't agree. It rains so much there in January and February. I can't stand it!

12.03

1 **A** I think the Amazon is the longest river in the world.
B I don't think so. Actually, I think the Nile is longer than the Amazon.
2 **A** Swiss chocolate is much better than British chocolate.
B You're absolutely right. It's probably the best in the world.
3 **A** Russian is a harder language to learn than Spanish.
B That could be. In my opinion, Spanish is one of the easiest languages to learn.
4 **A** Everybody should retire when they reach 60.
B Oh, please. That's way too early! Older people have so much experience that they can pass on to their younger coworkers.
5 **A** Tablets are so much more practical than laptops.
B That's true. They're much lighter and easier to carry.
6 **A** His last movie was amazing!
B You're right. It's the best movie he's made so far.

12.04

1 **A** Antonio Banderas is a Mexican actor.
B Um, he's actually a Spanish actor.
2 **A** French food's the best in the world.
B Well, actually, I think Italian food is the best.
3 **A** I like the American English accent.
B Do you? I prefer British English, actually.
4 **A** New York's the best place to live in the U.S.
B Actually, I think San Francisco's the best place.
5 **A** I think Chelsea will win the Champions League this year.
B No way! Barcelona will win it this year.
6 **A** Baseball is the most popular sport in the Mexico.
B I'm sorry, but I think soccer is the most popular sport.

12.05

DIANA So, where have you been in India so far, Brad?
BRAD I flew into Delhi and took the train down across to Jaipur. I'm going to Goa next. Have you been there, Leo?
LEO Yeah, Goa's cool. We're going to Kerala. How's your trip been so far, Brad?
B Aside from the mosquitoes and the spiders, pretty good. I had a great time in Delhi. I stayed with this Indian guy, Raj, who I'd met through a couch surfing website. He was really sociable and took me to some really amazing places.
D Yeah, we've met some great Indian people. Really friendly and generous.
B Yeah, but not everyone. I had a pretty bad time in Jaipur.
D What happened?
B I met these two brothers, Jay and Vikram, in a tea house. Jay was really funny and confident. He knew a lot about California. Viki was older and a bit more sensible. They offered to show me around, and they seemed reliable, so I agreed. We went sightseeing, and they told me about their lives. Viki said that they could take me to see some tigers the next day if I wanted.
L Sounds cool.
B Well, then they started telling me about their business. They sold jewelry. They took me to their factory and showed me around. Then they tried to sell me some. I didn't want to, but in the end, I said I would buy a small piece. They said it would be ready the next day, and then took me back to my hostel. The next day I felt a little anxious, but I went to their factory to pick up the jewelry. They had made my piece and had made 30 other necklaces, too. They said that this was what I had asked for the day before. They told me that I would have to pay 100 dollars for the jewelry. I had only taken 10 dollars with me when I left that morning. Jay said that he would take me to a cash machine to get the money. I hadn't taken my debit card with me, but I didn't tell him that. We drove to a bank and we all got out. I didn't know where I was, but I decided to run away. I started running and Jay followed me. But I was faster, and after a few minutes I was safe. I waited behind a trash can on a small street for a while, and then went onto the main road and found a taxi. The driver could see how anxious I was and drove me back to the hostel. I told him what had happened, and he was pretty angry with them. He was really generous and didn't charge me anything. The next day I took the first train out of Jaipur!
L Sounds awful. But hey, that's a pretty cool story you have.
D Yeah.
B Yeah, I know. I'm sure you have some stories. And we have another three hours on this train!
L No worries, buddy. So, we were in Varanasi …

Unit 1

1A

1

a 2 serious 3 delicious 4 beautiful 5 silly 6 wonderful

b 2 delicious 3 perfect 4 strange 5 **B** all right 6 awful 7 amazing 8 rude

2

a 2 did you meet 3 Did he grow up 4 was the movie like 5 did you pay 6 Why did she go 7 did he make 8 was your vacation

b 2 Does he work in a bank?
3 Why did you go to New York last month?
4 What is that new Brazilian restaurant like?
5 Who was that man with your sister?
6 What kind of TV shows do you watch?
7 Which university did you go to?
8 How much did the tickets cost?

1B

1

a 2 I particularly enjoy watching old Hollywood movies.
3 She absolutely hates it when people are late for meetings.
4 We usually go to Italian restaurants, but sometimes we go to Mexican ones.
5 We're pretty sure his flight arrives at Terminal 2, but I need to check.
6 I really hope he brings his beautiful sister to the party!

b 2 hardly ever 3 usually 4 fairly 5 really 6 rarely 7 really 8 pretty

2

a long vowel: 1, 4, 6, 8, 10

3

a 2 go 3 'm reading 4 wants 5 are you waiting 6 visit 7 's studying 8 're playing

b 2 's buying 3 don't 4 send 5 write 6 post 7 don't use 8 sends 9 are Marco and Jack doing 10 're spending 11 doesn't like 12 's

1C

1

a 2 What a 3 to see you 4 these days 5 far from 6 how 7 this is 8 news 9 meet 10 too

c 2 news 3 need 4 surprise 5 hello 6 time 7 meet 8 call 9 again 10 last

2

a 2 nice, surprise 3 really, nice, meet 4 sorry, really, need 5 Where, living 6 late, meeting

1D

1

a c

b True: 2, 5; False: 1, 3, 4, 6

2

a 2 Yesterday we visited the Palace of Versailles near Paris.
3 In the mornings, I usually go to the beach with my Portuguese friends.
4 I hope you're having a great time in Canada with your family.
5 Their English is very good, but we always speak in German.

3

a **Suggested answer:**

Hi Paul,

Hope you're having a good vacation in Ireland.

I'm spending two weeks with my brother and his family here in Turkey. I don't speak Turkish, but my brother's wife and his three children speak very good English, so communication isn't a problem.

They live about 30 km from Istanbul in a small town on the Bosphorus. It's very hot right now, but there is a big swimming pool near their house, so we go swimming there every day.

I'm visiting a lot of amazing places with my brother's family. Yesterday we went to the Grand Bazaar in downtown Istanbul. It's an enormous indoor market and there are over 3,000 stores. I'm sending you a photo of it. I bought a beautiful leather bag.

My brother's house has a big yard, so we usually have dinner outside at night when it isn't so hot. We normally eat at about ten o'clock. My sister-in-law's a great cook, so the food is delicious!

I'm having a wonderful time in Turkey.

See you back at work next month.

Maria

Reading and listening extension

1

a 2 c 3 a

b 2 b 3 c 4 a 5 b

2

a 2 a 3 b

b 2 a 3 b 4 c 5 a 6 b

Review and extension

1

2 At the moment, she's working at the café by the bus station. / At the moment, she is working at the café by the bus station.
3 Why did you miss the bus?
4 I can't talk to you now because I'm doing my homework.
5 What kind of music do you usually listen to?
6 They're waiting for the bus to Dallas. / They are waiting for the bus to Dallas.

2

2 We really enjoyed the movie last night.
3 We had a wonderful time at the party last night.
4 I think our Italian class is so boring.
5 I think that man's a little strange. Look, he's talking to himself.
6 New York's all right, but I prefer to live in Los Angeles / New York is all right, but I prefer to live in Los Angeles.

3

2 h 3 a 4 c 5 g 6 f 7 b 8 d

Unit 2

2A

1

a 2 I slept very badly on the plane, so I felt very tired the next day.
3 Did you take the train from New York to Washington?
4 Correct
5 They spent two nights at a hotel, and then they stayed at a friend's house for three days.
6 I didn't enjoy my trip to New Orleans because the weather wasn't very good.
7 Correct
8 Correct

b 1 **B** didn't sleep, weren't 2 **A** did you do **B** didn't have, decided
3 **A** did Ben go **B** went 4 **A** Did you bring **B** did, bought
5 **A** Did you see **B** did, met 6 **A** Did you visit **B** didn't have

2

a 2 e 3 a 4 f 5 h 6 b 7 c 8 g

b 2 passport 3 backpack 4 guidebook 5 foreign currency 6 suitcase

3

a hated, sounded, posted, invited

2B

1

a 2 gave 3 left for 4 missed 5 took off 6 landed 7 boarded 8 changed 9 got to

b 1 **B** crash 2 **A** miss **B** got lost 3 **A** long delays **B** strike 4 something wrong 5 line, broke down 6 **B** turbulence

2

a 2 was snowing 3 Were you flying 4 were you driving 5 were you standing 6 wasn't working

b 2 was driving 3 broke down 4 missed 5 bought 6 were waiting 7 started 8 decided 9 took 10 bought

3

a /ʌ/: 2, 5, 6, 7
/ɜ/: 3, 4, 8

2C

1

a
2 Could you tell me where the information desk is?
3 How much is a round-trip ticket to Boston?
4 How often do the buses leave for the airport?
5 What time is the next train to Barcelona?
6 Can I pay for my ticket in dollars?
7 Where can I buy a sandwich for the trip?
8 How much does it cost to get a taxi to the airport?

c 2 can 3 Could you 4 from 5 what time 6 anything else 7 Actually 8 near here 9 over there 10 Have

e 2 b 3 f 4 d 5 h 6 g 7 e 8 a

2

a 2 a 3 a 4 b 5 a 6 a

2D

1

a 1 d 2 c

b True: 2, 3, 5; False: 1, 4, 6

2

a 2 because 3 but 4 and 5 because 6 When 7 so 8 but

3

a **Suggested answer:**
Carlos and I got to New York at 10:30 last night. It was a very long flight from Quito, and we were very tired when we arrived because we couldn't sleep on the plane. When we got off the plane, the first thing we noticed was the cold – minus six degrees! It was freezing! Everything they say about New York is true! The people at the airport weren't very friendly, and we couldn't understand them because they spoke so quickly. In the end, we took the subway from JFK Airport to Manhattan. We're staying at the Crowne Plaza Hotel near Central Park. The hotel is full of European tourists, and everyone was very friendly and helpful. Carlos is telling me to get ready to go and eat, so I have to finish now – more tomorrow.

Reading and listening extension

1

a 2 a, c 3 a, d

b 2 Ben and Sam 3 Ben and Sam 4 Beto and Katie 5 Beto and Katie

c 2 sunny 3 ride 4 cost 5 afternoon

2

a 2 e 3 c 4 d 5 b

b 2 c 3 a 4 a 5 b 6 a

Review and extension

1

2 When we got to the station, the train was just arriving.
3 My wife called me while I was waiting for my plane.
4 A man took my wallet while I was waiting in line for my ticket.
5 Last year, we went on vacation to Costa Rica for two weeks.
6 I was driving to the airport when I saw the accident.

2

2 My trip from Miami to Memphis took 15 hours.
3 Last week, I went to Rome on a business trip.
4 The traffic was terrible because it was rush hour.
5 By the time they checked out of the hotel, it was 2 p.m.
6 In the afternoon, they went sightseeing in the old town.

3

2 cut 3 took 4 fell 5 75% 6 drove 7 I'm 8 are

Unit 3

3A

1

a
2 Have you ever been to carnival in Rio de Janeiro?
3 I bought a new TV and cell phone this month.
4 You have never borrowed money from me.
5 Have they ever done any volunteer work?
6 She has never left a big tip for a server.
7 Have you ever given any money to a homeless person?
8 I found several good bargains this month.

b
1 **B** gave
2 **A** Has she ever asked **B** asked
3 **A** Have you ever helped **B** helped
4 **A** 've left / have left **B** did you leave
5 **A** Has he ever bought **B** bought

2

a 2 g 3 a 4 h 5 e 6 c 7 d 8 b

b 2 into 3 bank account 4 afford 5 lend 6 borrow 7 spend 8 loan 9 back

3B

1

a 2 h 3 e 4 b 5 g 6 c 7 f 8 a

b 2 give 3 did 4 gave 5 do 6 made 7 doing 8 given

2

a 2 already 3 already 4 yet 5 already 6 yet 7 yet 8 already

b
2 He's already made a payment of $2,000.
3 Have you given your parents directions yet?
4 Eva has already given good advice.
5 I haven't made any new friends at school yet.
6 Has she done any volunteer work yet?
7 I've already bought a present for my wife.
8 They've already given $1,000 away to charity.

3C

1

a 8, 1, 6, 9, 10, 3, 2, 5, 4, 7

c 2 for 3 in 4 next 5 On second thought 6 enter 7 size 8 something else

d
2 I think I'm a size 14.
3 Do you have the same one in blue?
4 Can you tell me how much it is?
5 That's a little too expensive.
6 Do you have a cheaper one?

2

a 2 <u>en</u>ter, PIN 3 <u>pres</u>ent, <u>hus</u>band 4 black, jeans 5 Thanks, take 6 <u>Ac</u>tually, book

3D

1

a c

b True: 2, 3; False: 1, 4

2

a 7, 5, 2, 4, 1, 3, 6

3

a **Suggested answer:**
Hello everyone,
This email is to say a big "Thank you!" to everyone who helped us raise money for Save the Children over the past 12 months. We have successfully raised $495!
Most of you came to the Save the Children sports day in September. That was a great event and we all had a lot of fun. A lot of you also came to our 1990s karaoke night in October. And, of course, next week there's our popular quiz night with big prizes for the winning team.
Save the Children will use our money to save children's lives and to give them a better future. Last year, Save the Children helped ten million children around the world. A small amount can make a big difference. For example, just $3 can save the lives of eight children with a stomach virus.
Would you like to help us raise more money for Save the Children? Email us and we can tell you about our future events. Thanks again for all your help.

Reading and listening extension

1

a 2 100 3 13 million 4 12 million

b True: 1, 3, 5; False: 2, 4

c 2 wrote 3 cost 4 spend 5 get 6 borrow 7 save 8 bought

2

a 2 Anita 3 Mike 4 Anita 5 Gary

b 2 b 3 a 4 b 5 c 6 b

Review and extension

1

2 Have you ever given money to charity?
3 I went to China on business last year.
4 I've just bought a new cell phone. / I have just bought a new cell phone.
5 I haven't bought a birthday present for my brother yet.
6 I've already spent $200 this weekend. / I have already spent $200 this weekend.

2

2 Can you lend me 50 dollars, please?
3 I don't have a credit card, so I always pay with cash.
4 James is saving up for a new computer.
5 Our taxi driver was very friendly, so we gave him a big tip.
6 I bought a new laptop on sale – it was only $250!
7 Have you ever done any volunteer work?
8 Tony owes me $50, but he hasn't paid me back yet.

3

2 in time 3 under 4 like 5 about 6 over 7 talked 8 a beginner

Unit 4

4A

1

a 2 tie 3 sweater 4 top 5 earrings 6 tights 7 tracksuit
8 underwear 9 sandals 10 high heels 11 bracelet 12 flats

2

a 2 Are you going to invite your cousin to your wedding?
3 They're not going to get married this year.
4 What are you going to do after college?
5 We're going to visit my relatives in Spain next year.
6 What are you going to wear to the party?

b 2 are 3 meeting 4 're taking 5 are 6 staying 7 's coming
8 're bringing 9 're not flying 10 'm meeting

3

a 2 gonna 3 going to 4 going to 5 gonna 6 gonna 7 going to 8 going to

4B

1

a 2 h 3 g 4 b 5 f 6 a 7 d 8 e

b 1 **B** 'll 2 **B** 'll 3 should 4 won't 5 **A** Should **B** 'll 6 won't
7 Would 8 **B** Would

2

a Across: 5 indoor 7 high 8 ordinary 10 peaceful
Down: 1 modern 2 narrow 3 magnificent 6 noisy 9 huge

b 2 pretty 3 outdoor 4 quiet 5 modern 6 high

3

a 2 won't 3 won't 4 want to 5 want to 6 won't

4C

1

a 3, 10, 5, 2, 1, 6, 7, 4, 9, 8

c 2 Are you doing anything this Saturday?
3 This week's really busy for us.
4 What time should we come over?
5 What are you doing next Tuesday?
6 Would you like to come over for lunch?
7 I can't do Thursday this week.
8 Is this Sunday OK for you?

e 2 my mom 3 to the movies 4 work conference 5 at Diablo Lake
6 Saturday

2

a 2 meet, station 3 didn't, understand 4 hasn't, seen, movie
5 have, start, dinner 6 don't, like, basketball

4D

1

a d

b True: 2, 4; False: 1, 3, 5

2

a 2 Thanks for inviting me to your party.
3 It would be great to see you.
4 We're free on Saturday and we'd love to come.
5 We're having a party on Saturday.
6 We haven't seen you in ages!

3

a **Suggested answer if she can go:**
Hi Sam,
Nice to hear from you. Yes, I'm fine, thanks. My new job is great, but I'm working very hard.
Thanks for inviting me to your birthday party. I'm free next Saturday, and I'd love to come. Don't worry. I'll bring a huge salad! I'm looking forward to seeing you.
All the best,
Jess

Suggested answer if she can't go:
Hi Sam,
Nice to hear from you. Yes, I'm fine, thanks. My new job is great, but I'm working very hard.
Thanks for inviting me to your birthday party on Saturday. I'm really sorry, the party sounds like fun, but I'm afraid I can't come. I'd love to come, but I'm visiting my cousin in Vancouver next weekend.
Hope you have a nice birthday party. See you soon.
Love,
Jess

Reading and listening extension

1

a 6, 4, 5, 3, 2, 1

b True: 2, 3, 5; False: 1, 4

c 2 going to have, hasn't bought / has not bought
3 is going to / 's going to
4 is getting ready / 's getting ready
5 is arriving / 's arriving

2

a 2 Alex 3 Gavino 4 Marlon's mom 5 Isaac

b 2 b 3 b 4 c 5 b

Review and extension

1

2 Don't worry. I will pay the money back tomorrow. / Don't worry. I'll pay the money back tomorrow.
3 He's going to buy a new car next month. / He is going to buy a new car next month.
4 Should I come to your house in half an hour?
5 Should we go to that café for some coffee?
6 Are you going to do your homework tonight?

2

2 Are you going to buy a new suitcase on sale?
3 I love it here in the country. It's so peaceful!
4 He always wears a tie when he goes on a job interview.
5 I love coming to this park because you can't hear the traffic. It's so quiet here.
6 That restaurant's so noisy. It's really hard to talk there.

3

2 for 3 forward 4 good 5 around 6 up

Unit 5

5A

1

a 2 hairdresser 3 plumber 4 scientist 5 banker 6 electrician 7 lawyer 8 accountant 9 chef 10 nurse

b 2 salary 3 training 4 environment 5 team 6 college degree 7 people 8 self-employed 9 skills 10 qualifications

2

a 2 can't 3 can't 4 have to 5 have to 6 can't

b 2 can't 3 don't have to 4 have to 5 doesn't have to 6 has to 7 has to 8 must not 9 has to 10 doesn't have to

5B

1

a 2 h 3 a 4 g 5 b 6 f 7 e 8 d

b 2 might 3 won't 4 might not 5 will / 'll 6 **A** will / 'll **B** will 7 might 8 won't

2

a 2 construction worker 3 computer programmer 4 vet 5 designer 6 architect 7 musician 8 actor 9 journalist 10 taxi driver 11 sales assistant 12 politician

b 2 construction worker 3 musician 4 architect 5 sales assistant 6 actor 7 caregiver 8 computer programmer 9 journalist 10 designer 11 taxi driver 12 politicians

5C

1

a
2 Maybe you should ask your manager for the day off.
3 I'll look up the train times online.
4 Do you want me to call a taxi for our guest?
5 Why don't I drive you to the airport?
6 How about arranging a meeting in Mexico City?
7 Why don't you borrow some money from your dad?
8 You could catch a direct flight to Quebec.

c 1 **B** idea 2 **A** Would **B** fine, worry 3 **B** mind 4 **A** sorry **B** matter 5 about 6 don't 7 Maybe 8 could

2

a 2 stressed 3 unstressed 4 stressed 5 unstressed 6 stressed 7 unstressed 8 stressed

5D

1

a c

b True: 1, 3, 4, 6; False: 2, 5

2

a 2 f 3 d 4 a 5 h 6 c 7 b 8 e

3

a **Suggested answer:**
Dear Sir/Madam,
I am writing to apply for the job of sales assistant, which you advertised in *The Daily* newspaper.
I am a student at the University of North Carolina, and I am available to work starting in October.
A job with you will be an exciting opportunity for me to learn new skills and to work in a new environment. I have a lot of experience working in sales. Last summer, I worked for three months in a very busy store selling cell phones and computers, and I think this experience will be very useful in this job.
My résumé is attached with more details about my previous employment.
Could you give me more information about the salary and working hours, and also more details about your training program?
I look forward to hearing from you.
Sincerely,

Reading and listening extension

1

a 1 a 2 c 3 d 4 b

b
2 is doing something they love
3 gets paid well, is doing something they love, (sometimes) has to work many hours every day
4 gets paid well, works and studies, is doing something they love, has to work many hours every day

c 2 b 3 a 4 c 5 a, d

2

a 2 Construction worker, Hairdresser, IT worker, Bank teller 3 Hairdresser 4 IT worker, Bank teller 5 IT worker, Bank teller

b
1 early
2 skills, people/customers/clients
3 starting, weekends

Review and extension

1

2 Excuse me, sir. You can't eat in the laboratory. It's against the rules. / Excuse me, sir. You must not eat in the laboratory. It's against the rules.
3 Do you have to wear a suit to work?
4 When I finish school, I might go to college. It depends on my grades. / When I finish school, I may go to college. It depends on my grades.
5 I have to start work at 7 o'clock in the morning at my new job!
6 I'll take my umbrella. It might rain this afternoon. / I'll take my umbrella. It may rain this afternoon.

2

2 My sister works as a sales assistant in a big department store.
3 You need good qualifications if you want to become a doctor.
4 He works as a designer for a top fashion magazine.
5 If you want to become a plumber, you'll need to do a training program.
6 My brother wants to become a professional musician.

3

2 job 3 work 4 work 5 work 6 work 7 work 8 jobs 9 work

Unit 6

6A

1

a 2 go 3 Don't sit 4 shouldn't have 5 Eat 6 shouldn't drink 7 don't use 8 should read 9 should have 10 should go

b
2 Eat a lot of fruit and vegetables every day. / You should eat a lot of fruit and vegetables every day.
3 Don't use your computer for very long at night. / You shouldn't use your computer for very long at night.
4 You should try to relax for an hour before you go to bed. / Try to relax for an hour before you go to bed.
5 I think she should get more exercise during the day.
6 You shouldn't go swimming immediately after lunch.
7 When you have a headache, drink water. / When you have a headache, you should drink water.
8 Don't stay at work after six o'clock.

2

a 2 h 3 d 4 g 5 f 6 a 7 b 8 c

b 2 on 3 for 4 about 5 for 6 on 7 from 8 for

3

a 2 /u/ 3 /u/ 4 /ʊ/ 5 /u/ 6 /ʊ/ 7 /ʊ/ 8 /u/

6B

1

a 2 exciting 3 interested 4 shocked 5 annoyed 6 tiring 7 amazing 8 embarrassed

b 2 confused 3 interesting 4 surprising 5 frightened 6 disappointed 7 shocking 8 excited

2

a
2 It was interesting to learn about sharks.
3 Can you tell us where to park our cars?
4 It is dangerous not to wear a seat belt.
5 She took a bath to help her relax.
6 They went to the bus station to meet their aunt.
7 She called her father to ask him for some money.
8 He didn't know what to wear to the party.

b
2 He asked me how to get to the airport.
3 She was annoyed not to receive an invitation to his wedding.
4 They went to the supermarket to buy some food for dinner.
5 We couldn't remember which bus to catch to the airport.
6 John and Angela decided not to have their wedding in Hawaii.
7 It was embarrassing to fail my driving test again.
8 She went to the library to borrow a book on dinosaurs for her son.

6C

1

a 2 e 3 f 4 g 5 c 6 h 7 a 8 b

c
2 I think you should ask your coworkers.
3 I'm really sorry to hear that.
4 Do you think I should look for a new job?
5 I think it's a good idea to talk to your boss.
6 I'd talk to your parents about it.
7 I wouldn't apply for the new marketing job.
8 I don't think you should leave your job.

2

a 2 a 3 b 4 b 5 a

6D

1

a c

b True: 3, 5; False: 1, 2, 4

2

a
2 It's a good idea to read something in English every day. For example, you can read different newspapers online.
3 Why don't you do something relaxing this evening, such as going for a swim after work?
4 There are more enjoyable ways to prepare for an exam. For example, you could study with a friend who's in the same class.
5 You could start a new hobby to help you relax, such as dancing or swimming.

3

a **Suggested answer:**

Dear Kento,

Thanks for your message. I'm glad that you've written to me asking for some ideas.

I remember when I was learning Japanese, listening was the most difficult thing for me, too. I could understand when my teacher was talking to me, but it was very hard to understand when other people were speaking. Here are some ideas to help you improve your listening in English.

First of all, don't worry if you don't understand every word you hear. That's impossible! You should concentrate only on the most important words. Second, try to get extra listening practice outside the classroom. For instance, you can go to the learning center and practice listening with their listening exercises, such as the listening tracks from your Student's Book. You should also listen to the radio in English and watch English or American TV. It's a good idea to watch movies with the subtitles.

Next, you can also practice listening to podcasts. It's easy to download short stories onto your computer or phone. Finally, it's a good idea to listen to pop songs while you read the words at the same time. There are lots of websites that give you the words of the most popular pop songs.

I hope this helps and please feel free to talk to me after class next week.

Good luck,

Tina

Reading and listening extension

1

a 2 Petra 3 Petra 4 Petra 5 customers 6 Eva

b 2 b 3 a 4 c 5 c

c 2 b 3 a 4 d 5 e

2

a 2 Madison 3 Max 4 Elena 5 Max

b 2 c 3 c 4 b 5 b 6 a

Review and extension

1

2 I think he should do some exercise every day.
3 You should read a book to help you relax.
4 She asked me to drive her to the train station.
5 My father taught me how to play the guitar.
6 What should I do if I can't sleep well?

2

2 I was thinking about that TV show I saw last night.
3 My uncle paid for the tickets and bought popcorn for us as well.
4 I can't afford to spend a lot of money on a vacation this year.
5 My little sister isn't very interested in fashion.
6 I didn't hear the phone because I was listening to some music.
7 I didn't think that horror movie was frightening. What about you?
8 I didn't have any money, so I had to borrow $20 from my brother.

3

2 lent 3 brought 4 wrote 5 paid 6 read 7 sold 8 described

Unit 7

7A

1

a 2 hottest 3 colder 4 cold 5 smallest 6 big 7 larger 8 more expensive

b
2 I think it's the most exciting movie I've ever seen.
3 My sister is happier than she's ever been.
4 It's hard to understand her because she speaks more quickly than you.
5 He went to one of the best universities in the U.S.
6 The weather's much warmer than it was yesterday.
7 She worked harder than her sister and got 95% on her exam.
8 He speaks English much better now than a year ago. / Now he speaks English much better than a year ago. / He speaks much better English now than a year ago.

2

a 2 get in touch with 3 got a job 4 got to know 5 got together 6 get sick 7 get paid 8 got divorced

b 2 got married 3 got engaged 4 get accepted 5 got rich 6 got an offer 7 got to know 8 got paid

7B

1

a 2 f 3 g 4 b 5 d 6 a 7 h 8 e

b 2 put on, healthy 3 gone, lose 4 get 5 gave up 6 overweight 7 allergies 8 smoker

2

a 2 We didn't use to have 3 we didn't use to go 4 we used to invite 5 he used to cook 6 we used to watch 7 used to play 8 didn't use to complain 9 Did you use to live 10 did you use to live

b 2 didn't use to buy 3 did, use to eat 4 used to speak 5 used to take 6 Did, use to play 7 didn't use to have 8 used to watch

7C

1

a 2 g 3 h 4 e 5 f 6 c 7 a 8 b

c 2 hear 3 hurts, get 4 look 5 taking 6 sick 7 you 8 problem 9 relief 10 shouldn't

e 6, 8, 3, 1, 5, 4, 2, 7

2

a 2 down 3 up 4 down 5 down 6 up 7 up 8 up

7D

1

a c

b True: 2, 5; False: 1, 3, 4

2

a 2 After 3 Soon 4 a while 5 Then 6 the end

3

a **Suggested answer:**

About two years ago, I used to travel to work every day by bus. It was an awful ride because of all the traffic and sometimes it took me over an hour to get there. So I decided that I needed to find a quicker way to travel to work. I decided to buy a bicycle. The problem was that I wasn't very fit.

I bought an old bicycle from a friend of mine. At first, I was frightened of riding the bike on the road with all the cars and trucks. To begin with, I took my bike to the little park near my house every day and rode very slowly for about five or ten minutes. After a while, I started riding my bike along the quiet roads to the stores about two kilometers from my house. Then I started biking the five kilometers from my house to downtown. In the end, I went everywhere on my bicycle!

Now I ride eight kilometers to work every day, and I feel really fit and healthy. It only takes me 30 minutes to get to work, so I save an hour every day.

Reading and listening extension

1

a 2 a 3 d 4 b

b 2 used to be, in the past 3 used to have, in the past
4 used to smoke, in the past 5 are, now

c 2 a 3 c 4 b 5 c

2

a 2 Martin Dowd 3 Nick Downes 4 Brian Ramirez 5 Lisa Baker

b 2 smoking, drinking 3 lost, thinner / healthier / fitter
4 married 5 richer / wealthier 6 like

Review and extension

1

2 I think São Paulo is the biggest city in Brazil.
3 My brother didn't use to like coffee when he was a teenager.
4 This exercise is easier than the last one.
5 I'm studying harder this year than last year.
6 San Francisco is the most expensive city in California.

2

2 You'll have to go on a diet if you want to lose weight.
3 My brother has a new job and gets paid very well.
4 She loves her boyfriend, and I think they'll get engaged soon.
5 While he was at college, he got to know Percem.

3

2 g 3 c 4 b 5 a 6 e 7 d

Unit 8

8A

1

a 2 album 3 classical music 4 architecture 5 novel 6 sculpture
7 photograph 8 painting

b 2 M 3 L 4 A 5 L 6 A

2

a 2 wasn't made / was not made 3 was designed 4 was given
5 were finished 6 were made 7 was designed 8 was found
9 was created 10 were taken 11 was put 12 was finished
13 is visited

b 2 The Eiffel Tower was built in 1889.
3 The novel *Nineteen Eighty-Four* was written in 1948 by George Orwell. / The novel *Nineteen Eighty-Four* was written by George Orwell in 1948.
4 The 2012 Olympic Games were held in London.
5 The movie *Schindler's List* was directed by Steven Spielberg in 1993. / The movie *Schindler's List* was directed in 1993 by Steven Spielberg.
6 The best coffee is grown in Colombia.
7 Over 17 million new cars were sold in the U.S. in 2018. / Over 17 million new cars were sold in 2018 in the U.S.
8 Five thousand bicycles are produced by this factory every year. / Five thousand bicycles are produced every year by this factory. / Every year, 5,000 bicycles are produced by this factory.

8B

1

a 1 **B** 've loved / have loved, since
2 **A** Have you lived, for **B** 've lived / have lived
3 **A** have you been **B** 've been / have been, since, 've known / have known, for
4 **A** have you had **B** 've had / have had, since
5 **A** have you worked **B** 've been / have been, for

b 2 've known 3 's been 4 's had 5 've been, worked 6 's had

2

a play: squash, golf, volleyball, tennis, basketball, soccer, ice hockey
go: surfing, snowboarding, ice skating, jogging, rock climbing, skateboarding, scuba diving, windsurfing
do: yoga, track and field, aerobics, karate, judo

c Across: 4 volleyball 6 windsurfing 8 climbing 9 tennis 10 yoga;
Down: 1 hockey 2 snowboarding 3 golf 5 jogging 7 diving

3

a 2 a 3 a 4 b 5 a

8C

1

a 2 I'm sorry, I couldn't come to your party yesterday because I was sick.
3 I couldn't email you because my Wi-Fi wasn't working.
4 I didn't mean to be late for the meeting, but the train was delayed.
5 I'm really sorry I didn't buy you a present, but the stores were closed.
6 I'm sorry I didn't call you last night, but my phone wasn't working.
7 I was going to finish the report by today, but I've been so busy.
8 I meant to send you a birthday card, but I couldn't find your address.

b 2 couldn't 3 mean 4 matter, fine 5 going to 6 meant
7 worry, fault 8 had to

2

a 2 down 3 up 4 down 5 down 6 up 7 up 8 down

b More to say: 1, 3, 6, 7

8D

1

a c

b True: 1, 4, 5; False: 2, 3

2

a 2 However 3 although 4 However 5 Although 6 although

3

a **Suggested answer:**

War Horse by Michael Morpurgo is the story of Joey, a horse that is sold to the British Army at the beginning of World War I. He is sent to France and is ridden by Captain Nicholls. However, Captain Nicholls is killed in the fighting, and Joey is given to a younger soldier named Warren. While he is with Warren, Joey becomes friends with another horse named Topthorn, and they have a lot of adventures during the war. Later in the story, Joey and Topthorn are taken by the Germans. Topthorn is killed, but Joey works for the German army until the end of the war.

Although this book was written for children, I really enjoyed it. The story is very interesting, and the characters are described very well. You can really imagine what World War I was like. It's a beautiful story, although it's also really sad and it made me cry. However, there is a happy ending because at the end of the war, Joey is returned to Albert, who was his original owner before he was sold to the army. I couldn't put the book down until I got to the end, and I would definitely recommend it.

Reading and listening extension

1

a True: 1, 2, 5; False: 3, 4

b 2 Sam Lee 3 *To Sleep To Dream* 4 *Flathampton* 5 *To Sleep To Dream, Flathampton*

c 2 a 3 c 4 b 5 a

2

a 2 Stirling Ranges 3 Margaret River 4 Bunbury 5 near Fremantle 6 Stirling Ranges, Bunbury, Margaret River

b 2 The ocean 3 movie directors 4 listen to 5 Jenny

Review and extension

1

2 I have known Veronica since I was a child. / I've known Veronica since I was a child.
3 We've lived in Guayaquil for more than ten years.
4 St. Paul's Cathedral was designed by Christopher Wren.
5 I taught at that university from 2016 to 2019.
6 I have played golf since I was 12 years old. / I've played golf since I was 12 years old.

2

2 Skateboarding is a great way for children to get fit.
3 Do you have a photograph of your girlfriend?
4 Let's play golf this afternoon.
5 These days, ice skating is popular in New York City during the winter.
6 When I was in school, I had to do gymnastics every Wednesday.
7 The *Mona Lisa* is one of the most famous paintings in the world.
8 Let's go surfing at the beach this afternoon.

3

2 the way 3 mistake 4 bus 5 heart 6 hand 7 far 8 next Monday

Unit 9

9A

1

a Across: 6 administration 7 education
Down: 1 psychology 2 drama 3 engineering 4 medicine 8 art

b 2 degree 3 essays 4 fail 5 study 6 handed 7 notes 8 accepted 9 get 10 pass

2

a
2 I'll go to Canada on vacation if I can find a cheap flight.
3 If they study every day, they might pass their exams.
4 If she does well on her exams, she might get accepted to Northwestern University.
5 She'll have to get excellent grades if she wants to study medicine in college.
6 I'll call him tomorrow morning if he doesn't reply to my email tonight.
7 Your teacher might give you a bad grade if you don't hand in your essay on time.
8 If you fail your exams, you won't get into college.

3

a
2 If you take notes in class, // it will be easier to study for the exam.
3 I'm going to work harder next year // so that I get better grades.
4 If she fails her exam, // she'll have to take it again in January.
5 Although he got excellent grades, // he didn't get accepted to Oxford University.

9B

1

a 2 not to take 3 trying 4 to see 5 not to fail 6 not taking 7 to speak 8 to go 9 spending 10 not doing

b 2 to take 3 going 4 to get 5 playing / to play 6 to meet 7 reading 8 snowing / to snow

2

a 2 recommended 3 disliked 4 forgot 5 agreed 6 imagined 7 missed 8 avoid 9 managed 10 regretted 11 seemed 12 refused

b 2 avoids 3 arrange 4 forgot 5 recommends 6 miss 7 refuse 8 disliked 9 seems 10 manage

9C

1

a 9, 7, 3, 2, 5, 4, 8, 1, 6, 10

c 2 it is 3 it's 4 good time 5 catch that 6 just saying 7 I have 8 call you back 9 need to go 10 Call 11 soon

2

a 2 a 3 a 4 b 5 a 6 b

9D

1

a c

b True: 1, 3; False: 2, 4, 5

2

a 2 They 3 She's 4 her 5 one 6 He, he 7 us 8 It, it

3

a **Suggested answer:**

Tell us about you ...
Hello, everyone. I'm Hitomi, and I come from Osaka, in Japan. I'm getting a master's degree in economics at Tokyo University, and next year I want to get a job in London or New York. I studied English for ten years at school, so I can write it pretty well, but I can't speak it very well, so I need to practice!

How do you feel about this online course?
I really want to learn more about American movies because I've always loved watching them. I hope the course will help me improve my English. I'm looking forward to talking about all the movies we're going to watch with the other students in the course. I'm sure my English will improve quickly during the course.

What do you do when you're not studying?
When I'm not studying, I play a lot of sports. I play tennis once or twice a week and sometimes golf on weekends. I also go to the gym at the university because I like keeping really fit. Sometimes I do yoga when I feel stressed. It really helps me relax.

Reading and listening extension

1

a 2 medicine 3 law 4 psychology

b 2 a 3 a 4 b 5 b

c 2 the U.S. 3 speaks 4 studying 5 work / a job

2

a True: 1, 2, 6; False: 3, 4, 5

b 2 f 3 e 4 a 5 c 6 d

Review and extension

1

2 I want you to buy me some bread and milk from the store.
3 We won't play golf this afternoon if it rains.
4 She enjoys reading books about dinosaurs.
5 Will you go to college next year if you get good grades?
6 I just finished having dinner with my family.

2

2 He did really well at school and got into a good college.
3 She got a very bad grade on her last history essay.
4 Although they worked hard, they both failed their math exams.
5 She always took taxis because she disliked waiting for buses.
6 He got a degree in medicine, and now he's a doctor.

3

2 away 3 down 4 off 5 on

Unit 10

10A

1

a 2 Would you complain if the server made a mistake with your check?
3 What would you do if there were no teachers at school?
4 If I rode my bike to work, I could save a lot of money on gas.
5 I would feel less stressed if I did yoga every day.
6 If I missed the last bus, I'd have to take a taxi.
7 I could stop working if I became rich.
8 If you found the movie on the Internet, would you download it?

b 2 Could you work, needed
3 were, I'd complain
4 I could take, weren't
5 walked, you'd feel
6 stopped, 'd take
7 wouldn't walk, were
8 would you do, lost

2

a 2 g 3 d 4 c 5 f 6 e 7 b 8 a

b 2 off 3 over 4 like 5 up 6 in 7 of 8 on

3

a 2 unstressed 3 stressed 4 stressed 5 unstressed 6 stressed

10B

1

a 2 a little 3 no 4 much 5 much 6 many 7 many 8 any 9 a few 10 any 11 some

b 2 too much 3 enough milk 4 too 5 clearly enough 6 too many 7 too quickly 8 big enough

2

a Across: 6 decision 8 delivered 9 complaint 10 complain
Down: 1 choose 2 decided 4 description 5 enjoy 7 explain

3

a 2 b 3 b 4 a 5 b 6 a 7 b 8 b

10C

1

a 7, 1, 4, 2, 6, 5, 8, 3

c 2 I'll ask someone to look at that for you right away.
3 We've been here for over an hour, but we still haven't ordered.
4 These shoes don't fit me because they're a little small.
5 I've changed my mind, and I've decided to keep it.
6 I'd like to exchange it for something else.
7 I'd like to return this watch, please.
8 I'll give you a full refund.
9 Your sales assistant hasn't been very helpful.

2

a 2 b 3 a 4 b 5 b 6 a 7 b 8 a

10D

1

a 1 Email C 2 Email A 3 Email B

b True: 1, 4; False: 2, 3, 5

2

a 2 Thank you very much for your email of June 15.
3 I am writing to apologize for the poor service you received in our restaurant last Saturday.
4 We have just opened the restaurant, and we have had a few problems finding experienced servers.
5 However, we are working hard to improve our levels of service, and I am confident that we will not have any more problems like this in the future.
6 We hope you will come back to our restaurant again, and we would like to offer you a 50% discount on your next meal with us.
7 This is our way of apologizing for the problems you have had.
8 Sincerely,

3

a **Suggested answer:**

Dear Mr. Hurst,

Thank you for your email of July 10 about the problems you had during your stay at our hotel. I am writing to apologize for the poor service you had while you were staying with us.

Unfortunately, we have had a few problems with our website recently. I think that is why you were not given a room with an ocean view. We have also had some problems with our water heating system in the last few weeks, so this is why sometimes there was not enough hot water for showers or baths. Finally, we did not have enough staff in our restaurant while you were staying with us because three of our servers became sick.

I hope you will come and stay at our hotel in Cartagena again. I would like to offer you a 50% discount the next time you come to the Hotel Dante. This is our way of apologizing for the problems you have had.

Sincerely,

Fabián García

Manager

Hotel Dante

Reading and listening extension

1

a 2 c 3 a

b 2 a 3 b 4 a 5 b

c 2 b 3 b 4 c 5 a 6 a, b 7 c 8 c

2

a 2 Zuza 3 Zuza 4 No one 5 Haluk 6 Zuza

b 2 c 3 c 4 b 5 b 6 c

Review and extension

1

2 He invited too many people to his party – over 100!
3 If I had a motorcycle, I wouldn't take the bus to work.
4 This morning it was too cold to swim in the ocean.
5 I would go on a diet if I were overweight. / I'd go on a diet if I were overweight.
6 If Chile won the World Cup, he would be delighted.

2

2 Tim isn't here right now, but I can pass on a message.
3 There's a very small menu in that restaurant, so the choice of food is very limited.
4 It's sad that Anna and Esteban have broken up after being together for ten years.
5 If you're not happy with your hotel, you should make a complaint. / If you're not happy with your hotel, you should complain.
6 She was offered a better job, but she turned it down.

3

2 go 3 put 4 keeps 5 put 6 keep 7 got 8 kept

Unit 11

11A

1

a 2 where 3 which 4 who 5 where 6 who 7 which 8 which 9 where 10 who

b 2 There's a woman over there that used to work for your company. / There's a woman over there who used to work for your company.
3 There's a café near me which has 50 different kinds of tea! / There's a café near me that has 50 different kinds of tea!
4 My dad has a cousin in Houston who works for NASA. / My dad has a cousin in Houston that works for NASA.
5 I know an Italian restaurant in London where you can have chocolate spaghetti!
6 I have a new phone which also comes with free music apps. / I have a new phone that also comes with free music apps.
7 That's the movie theater where they're showing the new Superman movie next week.
8 He just bought a new TV which has amazing picture quality. / He just bought a new TV that has amazing picture quality.

2

a Across: 4 science fiction 5 theater 8 road sign 11 rock stars
Down: 1 series 2 coffee 4 soundtrack 6 address 7 lights 9 screen 10 cars

3

a 2 computer screen 3 science fiction 4 address book 5 bread knife
6 parking lot 7 coffee cup 8 bookshelf

11B

1

a 2 a 3 a 4 Ø 5 a 6 Ø 7 Ø 8 Ø 9 the 10 the 11 a 12 the
13 Ø 14 Ø 15 the 16 Ø 17 the 18 the 19 the 20 Ø 21 the
22 the

c
2 In the U.K., police officers don't usually carry guns.
3 I love Italian ice cream. It's the best in the world!
4 They drove to Paris by car and then stayed in a beautiful hotel near the Eiffel Tower.
5 France is the most popular country for tourists in the world.
6 Doctors in the U.S. are paid much more than nurses.

2

a 2 g 3 a 4 d 5 b 6 e 7 h 8 c

b 2 Unfortunately 3 by chance 4 Luckily 5 on purpose 6 Amazingly

3

a 2 a 3 b 4 b 5 a 6 b 7 a 8 a 9 b

11C

1

a 4, 6, 1, 3, 5, 2

c
2 Go through those doors and then down the corridor.
3 So, first go down the corridor to the stairs?
4 Could you tell me where the staff lounge is, please?
5 Then go down the corridor, and it's the first office on the right.
6 Go up the stairs to the third floor.
7 So, can I just check?
8 OK, I think I got it.
9 At the top of the stairs, turn right and go down another corridor.
10 The meeting room is the second door on the left.

2

a /ɜr/: 2, 5, 7
/eər/: 3, 4, 6, 8

11D

1

a b

b True: 1, 3, 5; False: 2, 4

2

a 2 since 3 because 4 because of 5 Since 6 as a result of
7 Because of 8 because

3

a **Suggested answer:**
In my opinion, the most important invention of the last 25 years has been the cell phone. Before it was invented, if you wanted to speak to somebody on the phone, you had to be at home, in the office, or in a public phone booth. With a cell phone, it is much easier to keep in contact with your friends, your family, and your coworkers than before. You can have a conversation wherever you are – on the street, at the supermarket, in a car, or on a train. Because of this, it is also easier for people to stay in touch with their children or with their elderly relatives. It is also very useful to have a cell phone if you have an accident or if you need to call the police. These days, cell phones are not only devices that let you make phone calls and send texts. You can also take photos, record videos, listen to music, surf the Internet, and talk to your friends on Facebook. I believe it's the most useful thing I have. In fact, I don't know where I would be without it.

Reading and listening extension

1

a 2 plane / airplane 3 rainforest / forest 4 candy 5 river 6 boat 7 hospital

b True: 1, 2; False: 3, 4, 5

c 2 b 3 e 4 c 5 a 6 f

2

a 5, 3, 6, 7, 4, 2, 1

b 2 a 3 c 4 a 5 b 6 b

Review and extension

1

2 Sorry, I can't talk to you right now because I'm at work.
3 Generally speaking, most men like watching sports on TV.
4 Modern Living is the store where I bought my leather sofa.
5 Look! That's the man who stole my wallet!
6 John F. Kennedy was the American president who was assassinated in Dallas in 1963. / John F. Kennedy was the American president that was assassinated in Dallas in 1963.

2

2 I think I wrote his phone number in my address book.
3 Surprisingly, it tasted a little like chicken.
4 I'm afraid of heights, so I don't want to go rock climbing.
5 He opened the car door without looking and hit an old man on a bicycle.
6 I'm sorry I broke your coffee cup – it was an accident.

3

2 a 3 e 4 d 5 b 6 c

Unit 12

12A

1

a Across: 5 camel 6 bee 7 parrot; Down: 1 spider 2 gorilla 4 whale 8 tiger

2

a 2 had, finished 3 had worked 4 had gotten up 5 had, begun 6 had stolen
7 had missed 8 had stopped

b 2 began 3 left 4 was 5 had crashed 6 was 7 reached 8 had missed
9 had taken 10 arrived 11 tried 12 had sold 13 bought 14 spent
15 landed 16 didn't collect 17 had been 18 found 19 had closed
20 went

3

a /ʌ/: come, done, run, won /ɔ/: talked, taught
/oʊ/: known, spoken, woken

12B

1

a
2 said, she would, me
3 told me, her, was watching, her
4 said, they'd gone, their
5 told him, his, couldn't, them
6 told us, thought, they would go, their
7 said, she'd already done, her
8 told us, his, wasn't going to, his

b
2 He told me he would invite us to his house for dinner next week. / He told me that he would invite us to his house for dinner next week.
3 She told James he could use her computer to do his homework. / She told James that he could use her computer to do his homework.
4 He said the traffic had been really bad, so they had missed the 5:15 train. / He said that the traffic had been really bad, so they had missed the 5:15 train.
5 She told me they were going to buy me a wonderful present for my birthday. / She told me that they were going to buy me a wonderful present for my birthday.
6 He said he had tried calling his friend, but she hadn't answered, so he thought she was away on vacation. / He said that he had tried calling his friend, but she hadn't answered, so he thought she was away on vacation.

2

a Across: 5 sociable 7 serious 8 shy 10 anxious
Down: 1 careless 3 selfish 4 generous 6 creative 9 funny

12C

1

a 2 d 3 e 4 c 5 a 6 b 7 h 8 f

c 2 **B** You're absolutely right. 3 **B** That could be. 4 **B** Oh, please.
5 **B** That's true. 6 **B** You're right.

2

a 2 Italian 3 British 4 San Francisco 5 Barcelona 6 soccer

12D

1

a d

b True: 2, 4; False: 1, 3, 5

2

a 2 Later that day 3 The next morning 4 By morning
5 A few hours later

3

a **Suggested answer:**
Last year, I went on a hiking trip in Utah with three of my friends. We had only been there for a day when the accident happened. We had just gotten to the top of a mountain, and we were eating some sandwiches that we'd made for lunch. A few minutes later, the weather changed completely. It had been a clear, sunny day when we left the town where we were staying. However, now it was snowing heavily, and you could only see clearly for about 20 meters. We started walking down the path toward the next town where we were going to spend the night. The snow was getting deeper, so we walked slowly down the mountain. All of us were confident hikers, so we didn't think we would have any problems. Suddenly, I heard a shout from behind me. When I turned around my friend Anthony was lying on the ground. He said that he had fallen over a rock. As soon as I saw him, I knew it was serious. He said his leg was hurting badly and that he thought he had broken it. We decided to call for help. Fortunately, my cell phone was getting a signal, so I managed to call the emergency services.

After a while, the mountain rescue team arrived in their helicopter. They landed very close to where we were. They carried Anthony to the helicopter, and we all got in with him. Ten minutes later, we arrived at the hospital. Luckily, Anthony's leg wasn't badly broken, and they didn't need to operate. By the next day, Anthony could leave the hospital. We all felt very relieved.

David

Reading and listening extension

1

a 4, 1, 5, 2, 6, 3

b 2 anxious, was worried about changing something
3 generous, gave a lot of money to buy something
4 sociable, friendly with people

c 2 a 3 b 4 c

2

a 6, 5, 1, 8, 4, 7, 2, 3

b 2 a 3 b 4 b 5 a 6 b

Review and extension

1

2 I told her that she couldn't go to the beach by herself. / I told her she couldn't go to the beach by herself. / I said that she couldn't go to the beach by herself. / I said she couldn't go to the beach by herself.
3 He told me that my mother had called earlier that day. / He told me my mother had called earlier that day. / He said that my mother had called earlier that day. / He said my mother had called earlier that day.
4 We told her that her father wouldn't buy her a new computer. / We told her her father wouldn't buy her a new computer. / We said that her father wouldn't buy her a new computer. / We said her father wouldn't buy her a new computer.
5 Tom had never ridden a camel before, so he was pretty nervous.
6 Our train had already left when we finally arrived at the station.

2

2 She's a really honest person. If sales assistants give her too much change, she always tells them.
3 He's very easygoing. I'm sure he won't mind if you bring your friend with you when you go to his house for dinner.
4 I'm not a very confident person. For example, I don't like speaking when I'm in a meeting with a large group of people.
5 Teachers have to learn to be patient with their students because sometimes they don't learn things immediately.
6 Why are you always so careless! You've already lost your cell phone twice this year!

3

2 At your age 3 old age 4 apart in age 5 at an early age
6 about my age

Acknowledgments

The authors and publishers acknowledge the following sources of copyright material and are grateful for the permissions granted. While every effort has been made, it has not always been possible to identify the sources of all the material used, or to trace all copyright holders. If any omissions are brought to our notice, we will be happy to include the appropriate acknowledgments on reprinting and in the next update to the digital edition, as applicable.

Key:
U = Unit

Photographs
All the photographs are sourced from Getty Images.

Front cover photography by YinYang/E+/Getty Images.

U1: Devasahayam Chandra Dhas/E+; Cavan Images; RoBeDeRo/E+; © Razvan Ciuca/Moment; Ugurhan/E+; Andresr/E+; Vladimir Vladimirov/E+; **U2:** Mixmike/iStock/Getty Images Plus; DavorLovincic/iStock/Getty Images Plus; Kenishirotie/iStock Editorial/Getty Images Plus; Mark Spowart/Moment; DenisTangneyJr/E+; Jouko van der Kruijssen/Moment; John Coletti/The Image Bank; **U3:** NurPhoto; Hill Street Studios/Stone; Eva-Katalin/E+; Photographer is my life./Moment; Peter Dazeley/The Image Bank; MicroStockHub/iStock/Getty Images Plus; Pollyana Ventura/E+; **U4:** Popovaphoto; Anterovium/iStock/Getty Images Plus; istanbulimage/E+; Tatniz/iStock/Getty Images Plus; ProArtWork; Popovaphoto/iStock/Getty Images Plus; Badahos/iStock/Getty Images Plus; Andrey Nikitin/iStock/Getty Images Plus; Adisa/iStock/Getty Images Plus; Pavel Skopich/EyeEm; Orchidpoet/E+; Stella Kalinina; Monkeybusinessimages/iStock/Getty Images Plus; Damircudic/E+; D3sign/Moment; Ippei Naoi/Moment; Christian Abate/EyeEm; Anton Aleksenko/iStock/Getty Images Plus; **U5:** Don Mason; izusek/E+; Ngampol Thongsai/Stock/Getty Images Plus; Fuse/Corbis; Scyther5/iStock/Getty Images Plus; Damircudic/E+; David Buffington/Photodisc; Dougal Waters/DigitalVision; DreamPictures/Photodisc; Mangostock/iStock/Getty Images Plus; Bambu Productions/The Image Bank/Getty Images Plus; Jupiterimages/PHOTOS.com/Getty Images Plus; Mint Images; Gavin Hellier/Robertharding; Maskot; P. Winbladh/The Image Bank; **U6:** Klaus Vedfelt/DigitalVision; Electravk/E+/Getty Images; Peathegee Inc; Fabrice LEROUGE/ONOKY; **U7:** Sen LI/Moment; FatCamera/E+; Bernardbodo/iStock/Getty Images Plus; Antonio_Diaz/iStock/Getty Images Plus; Wavebreakmedia/iStock/Getty Images Plus; Compassionate Eye Foundation/Steven Errico/DigitalVision; Orlando/Hulton Archive; **U8:** Bettmann; Olegback/iStock/Getty Images Plus; Gary Hershorn/Corbis News; Carol Yepes/Moment; Tim Graham/Getty Images News; Eric Feferberg/Afp; Just Nicolas/EyeEm; BraunS/E+; Matt Cardy/Getty Images News; Alphotographic/iStock; **U9:** Nycshooter/E+; PeopleImages/E+; Dramalens/iStock/Getty Images Plus; FG Trade/E+; Andresr/E+; Fstop123/E+; Commercial Eye/The Image Bank; **U10:** Monkeybusinessimages/iStock/Getty Images Plus; Maskot; FredFroese/E+; Graphixel/E+; Education Images/Universal Images Group; Hudiemm/DigitalVision Vectors; Peter Cade/Stone; Jeffrey Coolidge/Stone; **U11:** Rischgitz/Hulton Archive; Highwaystarz-Photography/iStock/Getty Images Plus; T2 Images/Cultura; C Squared Studios/Photodisc; Science & Society Picture Library; Mapodile/E+; Alblec/iStock/Getty Images Plus; Whitemay/E+; **U12:** PrinPrince/iStock; Michael England/Photodisc; Andresr/E+; BlackCAT/E+; Dimitrios Kambouris/Getty Images Entertainment; Yann Arthus-Bertrand/Getty Images Plus; Ryan Rombough; KeithBinns/E+; Parth Joshi/EyeEm.

The following photographs are sourced from other sources/libraries.

U8: Lebrecht Music & Arts; RTRO/Alamy Stock Photo; Wachiwit/Shutterstock.com.

Illustrations
QBS Learning; Mark Bird; Mark Duffin; Sean KJA; Jo Goodberry; Dusan Lakicevic; Carrie May; Jerome Mireault; Roger Penwill; Gavin Reece; Gregory Roberts; Martin Sanders; Sean Sims; Marie-Eve Tremblay; Javier Joaquin; Ben Swift.

Typeset by QBS Learning.

Audio Production by John Marshall Media.

Corpus
Development of this publication has made use of the Cambridge English Corpus (CEC). The CEC is a computer database of contemporary spoken and written English, which currently stands at over one billion words. It includes British English, American English and other varieties of English. It also includes the Cambridge Learner Corpus, developed in collaboration with the University of Cambridge ESOL Examinations. Cambridge University Press has built up the CEC to provide evidence about language use that helps us to produce better language teaching materials.

English Profile
This product is informed by English Vocabulary Profile, built as part of English Profile, a collaborative program designed to enhance the learning, teaching and assessment of English worldwide. Its main funding partners are Cambridge University Press and Cambridge Assessment English and its aim is to create a "profile" for English, linked to the Common European Framework of Reference for Languages (CEFR). English Profile outcomes, such as the English Vocabulary Profile, will provide detailed information about the language that learners can be expected to demonstrate at each CEFR level, offering a clear benchmark for learners' proficiency. For more information, please visit www.englishprofile.org.

CALD
The Cambridge Advanced Learner's Dictionary is the world's most widely used dictionary for learners of English. Including all the words and phrases that learners are likely to come across, it also has easy-to-understand definitions and example sentences to show how the word is used in context. The Cambridge Advanced Learner's Dictionary is available online at dictionary.cambridge.org.

CAMBRIDGE
UNIVERSITY PRESS

University Printing House, Cambridge CB2 8BS, United Kingdom

One Liberty Plaza, 20th Floor, New York, NY 10006, USA

477 Williamstown Road, Port Melbourne, VIC 3207, Australia

314–321, 3rd Floor, Plot 3, Splendor Forum, Jasola District Centre, New Delhi – 110025, India

103 Penang Road, #05-06/07, Visioncrest Commercial, Singapore 238467

Cambridge University Press is part of the University of Cambridge.

It furthers the University's mission by disseminating knowledge in the pursuit of education, learning and research at the highest international levels of excellence.

cambridge.org
Information on this title: cambridge.org/9781108818353

First published 2022

20 19 18 17 16 15 14 13 12 11 10 9 8 7 6 5 4 3 2 1

Printed in Poland by Opolgraf

A catalogue record for this publication is available from the British Library

ISBN 978-1-108-81812-4 Pre-intermediate Student's Book with eBook
ISBN 978-1-108-81851-3 Pre-intermediate Student's Book A with eBook
ISBN 978-1-108-81852-0 Pre-intermediate Student's Book B with eBook
ISBN 978-1-108-84969-2 Pre-intermediate Student's Book with Digital Pack
ISBN 978-1-108-84975-3 Pre-intermediate Student's Book A with Digital Pack
ISBN 978-1-108-84976-0 Pre-intermediate Student's Book B with Digital Pack
ISBN 978-1-108-81835-3 Pre-intermediate Workbook with Answers
ISBN 978-1-108-81836-0 Pre-intermediate Workbook A with Answers
ISBN 978-1-108-81837-7 Pre-intermediate Workbook B with Answers
ISBN 978-1-108-81838-4 Pre-intermediate Workbook without Answers
ISBN 978-1-108-81839-1 Pre-intermediate Workbook A without Answers
ISBN 978-1-108-81840-7 Pre-intermediate Workbook B without Answers
ISBN 978-1-108-81841-4 Pre-intermediate Full Contact with eBook
ISBN 978-1-108-81849-0 Pre-intermediate Full Contact A with eBook
ISBN 978-1-108-81850-6 Pre-intermediate Full Contact B with eBook
ISBN 978-1-108-84972-2 Pre-intermediate Full Contact with Digital Pack
ISBN 978-1-108-84973-9 Pre-intermediate Full Contact A with Digital Pack
ISBN 978-1-108-84974-6 Pre-intermediate Full Contact B with Digital Pack
ISBN 978-1-108-81853-7 Pre-intermediate Teacher's Book with Digital Pack
ISBN 978-1-108-81857-5 Pre-intermediate Presentation Plus

Additional resources for this publication at www.cambridge.org/americanempower

This page is intentionally left blank.

This page is intentionally left blank.

This page is intentionally left blank.

This page is intentionally left blank.